ELISHA

ELISHA

A SIGN
&
A WONDER

GREG HASLAM

Chariot Victor Publishing
A Division of Cook Communications

Chariot Victor Publishing,
a division of Cook Communications,
Colorado Springs, Colorado 80918
Cook Communications, Paris, Ontario
Kingsway Communications, Eastbourne, England

ELISHA: A SIGN AND A WONDER
© 1995 by Greg Haslam.

First U.S. edition, 1998
Printed in the United States of America.

Unless otherwise indicated, Biblical quotations are from the *New International
Version*, © 1973, 1978, 1984 by the International Bible Society.

Editor: Melissa Borger
Art Direction: Bill Gray
Design: Image Studios
Leader's Guide Editor: Carol Smith

1 2 3 4 5 6 7 8 9 10 Printing/Year 02 01 00 99 98

Library of Congress Cataloging-in-Publication Data

Haslam, Greg.
        Elisha: a sign and a wonder / [by Greg Haslam].
                p. cm. —(The Chariot Victor Bible character series)
        ISBN 1-56476-717-5
        1. Elisha (Biblical prophet)   I. Title. II. Series.
        BS580.E5H28 1998
        222' .54' 092–dc21
                                                                    98-20914
                                                                        CIP

Here am I and the children

whom the Lord has given me!

We are for signs and wonders in Israel

From the Lord of hosts,

Who dwells in Mount Zion

(Isaiah 8:18, NKJV)

The *Chariot Victor Bible Character* series introduces us to people in the Bible and shows how their lives have much to teach us today. All the authors in the series use their communication skills to lead us through the biblical record and apply its encouragements and challenges to our lives today. Every volume contains an *Index of Life Issues* to enhance its usefulness in reference and application.

Other books in the series:

Elijah: Anointed and Stressed by Jeff Lucas

CONTENTS

PREFACE

Today's bored consumers cruising the local shops on any Main Street require something truly eye-catching if they are to be persuaded to stop and look, let alone buy the display goods. Shop windows must grab attention if they are to invite the sales-resistant inside to see more. Yet who can ignore the well-dressed window of a toy shop at Christmas with its working models of road and rail amid full scenic layout? Similarly, most people will at least stop to notice the adorable puppy dogs as they tumble and play together in a pet shop window. People are drawn irresistibly to life, light, color, and movement. They only ignore the drab, dark, dead, and dirty.

The church is meant to be God's shop-front window display of what His kingdom is like. Local churches should be renowned for the life, joy, vitality, and power of their community life together. People should feel drawn at least to look, even to venture inside and find out exactly what we have to offer.

In Isaiah's day, the prophet faced dark times. True religion had declined and a strident paganism was on the increase. Isaiah's response was to gather a small community of disciples in whom he could invest his insights and power. He was confident that they would prove to be "signs and wonders in Israel" (Isa. 8:18 NKJV). They would act as indicators of better things to come. They would prove to be an occasion for astonishment in the eyes of a skeptical world.

We have got to become such a sign in our generation. I

truly believe that a study of the life of Elisha will help to show us how. The chapters which follow are meant to be both provocative and practical. They are designed to spell out some ways in which believers today can act as "signs and wonders" to a lost people in need of direction.

It is with real gratitude that I dedicate these studies to the faithful and enthusiastic congregation of Winchester Family Church who first heard them and with whom I have served God for fifteen years. They share my passion to become a "sign and wonder" to our contemporaries.

Since this book was written, we have enjoyed twelve months of the Holy Spirit's refreshing and renewal in common with thousands of other churches in the U.K. and across the world. These chapters seem peculiarly relevant at a time when so many are asking, "Where is it all leading?" and "What is it all for?" We all sense that something great is about to happen. Perhaps the next wave of blessing will be truly "tidal" in scale—revival itself. God is on the move. The church is being prepared for a major advance. We need to get ready, and the need is urgent.

May these studies on the life of Elisha serve to deepen our insight and involvement with all that the Lord is doing, and may we be provoked to become that glorious church which is "looking forward to the day of God" and eager also to "speed its coming" (2 Peter 3:12).

Greg Haslam
Pentecost 1995

INTRODUCTION
LET ME TELL YOU A STORY

Everybody loves a story, especially a good one. The story of Elisha, or perhaps we should say *stories* of Elisha, are by any reckoning good. It is surprising therefore how little they are known, and how little they are understood.

We need exposure to stories like these. Stories which grip us, bemuse us, move us, and fire us. Why have we ignored them for so long? It is not that this generation doesn't enjoy stories: novels sell in huge numbers, movies and videos are watched by millions, and television soaps are faithfully viewed episode by episode. This is so throughout the world.

It isn't that we are not interested in or affected by stories, it is simply that we are listening to the wrong ones. We live in a culture marked by lust, unfaithfulness, rebellion, instant gratification, broken relationships, hopelessness, escapism, depression, and futility. The stories we listen to all reflect and endorse this behavior. These stories share the bottom-up philosophies of despair held in common by all mankind. What we most need are stories which reflect the top-down theology of hope contained in the Bible.

There is tremendous power in the stories of Elisha. They intercept us in our fear-ridden wanderings, bringing us to the crossroads of sudden arrest and decision. We are called to question the meaning, direction, and purpose of our lives, to penetrate deeply the secret springs of our thoughts, convictions, and beliefs. They force us to examine all our assumptions. They expose us to an alternative worldview, a new perspective which makes sense for one basic reason—that these stories are true.

In these stories we identify with the characters and situations, with the emotions involved, the love, the loss, the joy, the pain. We know that these characters know what we know—that life is hard, intimidating, puzzling, and brief. And yet, in spite of these harsh realities, these personalities can show us, perhaps for the first time, how to live.

Much of the Bible consists of stories. Have you ever wondered why this is so?

The Bible does not deal in abstract, untried philosophical propositions, but in tried and proven realities. One of the best means of communicating these perspectives on ultimate reality is through stories. The writer of 2 Kings wanted us to learn a great deal of theology through a selection of these stories, and in the chapters which follow we will tap as much of that theology as we can. But don't forget that this theology is served to you through the very attractive means of some outstanding stories. This method of using stories to communicate theology was common in the world of the ancient Near East, and it is particularly the case in the Bible. God is a great storyteller; he seems to like this method of teaching very much. Why?

1. Stories are concrete

Since they concern particular people living in particular

times and places, stories lend themselves readily to meeting us in our own time and place. Cowardly preachers who are afraid of irritating or offending their hearers tend to deal in universal terms—they preach over people's heads and avoid everyone's gaze. But God fixes us with His gaze and, eyeball to eyeball, says, "This is for you!" He does this by telling us stories. It allows God to get specific with us. The scandal of specificity will mark a great deal of our examination of these stories.

2. Stories are pictorial

They fire our imaginations. We never tire of them because each time we read them they set our minds and our imaginations running in all sorts of directions. They seem to have endless applications because they have a timeless quality. They touch us with freshness at different periods of our lives. Listeners have freedom to decide for themselves what is going on each time they listen to the story. You will encounter forceful interpretation and application as you hear these stories recounted in this book, yet I hope that you never feel coerced as you submit yourself to them. You can let your imagination run free just as I did. We can both allow these images, metaphors, and symbols to work their way into our lives to the point in our experience where we receive them. God is taking all of us into His confidence when, with a loving arm around our shoulders and that intriguing whisper in His voice, He draws us closer to Himself and says, "Let me tell you a story. . . ."

3. Stories are unforgettable

Once God has planted these subversive images in your mind and told you something of their significance for your life, your church, your time, and your generation, then you can never again pretend that you have not heard them. These stories will ruin us. They spoil us for the kind of passive listening we are frequently engaged in: we cannot even watch the "soaps" or the latest Hollywood blockbusters in the same way as before. We have caught a glimpse into another world and so we interpret this world differently. We have seen beyond the barbed wire of the concentration camp in which most of our contemporaries live. We've caught a liberating glimpse of freedom, and we cannot help making trouble for the rest of the inmates who haven't yet seen what we've seen. Even if we get hurt doing this, or have to pay the ultimate price for reporting what we have both seen and heard, we cannot keep quiet. Walter Brueggemann describes the Bible in this way:

> Israel's narrative is a partisan, polemical narrative. It is concerned to build a counter community—counter to the oppression of Egypt, counter to the seduction of Canaan, counter to every cultural alternative and every imperial pretence. There is nothing in this narrative which will appeal to outsiders who belong to another consensus, or who share a different ethos and participate in another epistemology. To such persons, Israel's narratives are silly, narrow, scandalous, and obscurantist.[1]

Perhaps so, but not to us. To us they are photographs of true freedom, and we clutch them to our breasts. We guard them with our lives.

4. Stories are experiential

Like a good movie, the pacing of the narrative, the color, the movement, the life, the character development, and the accompanying musical score all draw us in. We are there. The story is told by participants and we cannot help but participate. Our lives are claimed. We find ourselves arrested, conscripted, convinced, commissioned, and equipped to become world-changers. But at the end of a film, we emerge into the cold night air able to shake off the temporary effect of the emotions we felt. Not so with Bible stories. We discover their unusual power to change our lives. We will never be the same again. We don't want to be the same again.

So be warned. You read these stories not to escape reality, but rather to find it. You are not about to enter the fantasy world of the *Arabian Nights* but the real world of God's defining. These stories are designed to help you come home; to return to reality after years in the unreal world of human or demonic fantasy and propaganda. As you read the history of Elisha, may I say in all seriousness, "Welcome to the real world!" These are God's castings of the solid blocks of reality. So solid, in fact, that if you walk into them you may hurt yourself. The effect may be startling.

The church today needs an awakening—a resurrection. At the end of the story of Elisha comes a remarkable incident. In 2 Kings 13:20-21 the narrator tells us that long after Elisha's death God used Elisha's bare bones to raise a dead Israelite to life. He still does. These stories represent the "bare bones" of Elisha's ministry, and Elisha's "bones" are still conveying life to dead Israelites. Just at the moment when people are saying "It's all over!" then God may say, "No, it's just about to begin." Whenever the world dances on the grave of the church, that's when God usually produces a resurrection. It has been my experience that these ancient stories still have power to awaken the dead. I hope you find this to be the case in your life also. You are about to meet a balding, wiry ex-farmer with calloused hands, a fearless countenance, a rasping tongue, and a heart of gold. Your life, perhaps, may never be the same again after the encounter.

---

1. Walter Brueggemann, *The Creative Word* (Fortress Press: Philadelphia, 1982), p. 27.

ELIJAH PASSES THE BATON

1 Kings 18:36-39; 19:13b-14, 19-21

Elijah prayed: "O Lord, God of Abraham, Isaac and Israel, let it be known today that you are God in Israel and that I am your servant and have done all these things at your command. Answer me, O Lord, answer me, so these people will know that you, O Lord, are God, and that you are turning their hearts back again." Then the fire of the Lord fell and burned up the sacrifice, the wood, the stones, and the soil, and also licked up the water in the trench. When all the people saw this, they fell prostrate and cried, "The Lord—he is God! The Lord—he is God! (1 Kings 18:36-39).

Then a voice said to him, "What are you doing here, Elijah?" He replied, "I have been very zealous for the Lord God Almighty. The Israelites have rejected your covenant, broken down your altars, and put your prophets to death with the sword. I am the only one left, and now they are trying to kill me too (1 Kings 19:13b-14).

The end is nigh

Is this the terminal generation? To listen to many observers—both secular and Christian—you would think so. They point to the many indicators of upheaval and urgent unrest: the earth's dwindling material resources, the ecological damage inflicted by man upon his environment, the sheer scale and global repercussions of the concerns reported in daily news. These events and the ferment in the spiritual and ideological perspectives of mankind all seem to confirm our worst suspicions. This widespread accumulation of alarming data seems not only to endorse the sober predictions voiced by Jesus and his apostles (see, for example, Matthew 24 and Revelation 8 and 9), they seem also to confirm what some had most feared—namely, that the church is in retreat, evil has triumphed, the Christian cause is all but lost, and the people of God are becoming an increasingly shrinking minority. The church appears besieged and beleaguered. Her only hope is said to lie in death or translation, resurrection or rapture. It doesn't really matter which, so long as it is an escape from the mess. That, at any rate, is what many sincerely believe and hope for.

Interestingly, it is also what the prophet Elijah believed and hoped for. The famous contest on Mount Carmel in which Yahweh's representative had rallied the forces and faith of his nation in the notable "power encounter" with the demonic fertility gods of Canaan, had ended with the utter supremacy of Yahweh being mounted in vivid and indisputable display. That night, 850 prophets of the discredited god Baal and his consort Asherah had all been brought to the Kishon Valley and persuaded to give blood in much larger amounts than those voluntarily donated earlier in the day (see 1 Kings 18:40 and 18:28). Elijah must surely have expected that the repentance of King Ahab, the renunciation of his demon-worshiping queen Jezebel, and the renewal of the people would all immediately follow. In fact, none of this happened. Instead, the nation just went home and told each other what an

18

exciting day it had been, Ahab went home and told Jezebel what a naughty boy Elijah had been and Jezebel went "ballistic" and after telling her gods what a loyal witch she had been, promptly put a contract out on Elijah's life.

Disappointment and disillusionment

Elijah could not have been more devastated. Alone, afraid, and disillusioned, he fled to the desert and, almost suicidal with disappointment and self-pity, he gave voice to the same convictions and aspirations of many believers today: "I have had enough, Lord . . . Take my life; I am no better than my ancestors . . . I am the only one left, and now they are trying to kill me too" (1 Kings 19:4, 10). It's the same desire for escape, resurrection, or rapture which marks so many sectors of the church today. This is a self-serving response, unworthy of a man with something more than a contract on his life—Elijah had the call of God on his life. He seemed to have forgotten that. His life was in danger and he thought that all was lost.

But Elijah was wrong. This wasn't the end, he wasn't the only one left and God's cause was by no means lost. Instead, God was at pains to point out that while Elijah's exhaustion and mood were to some degree understandable, in fact he had no business being where he was. "What are you doing here, Elijah?" (1 Kings 19:9) was not so much an inquiry about his location, as a challenge to both his frustration and resignation. God was mildly rebuking his defeatism and despair. The Lord took him to task for the narrowness of his perspective and the smallness of his vision.

Something similar needs to happen to us today. We too need to be told to stop complaining and get on with the work at hand. Immediate escape is not an option. It is better to think long term and to look beyond our own minor (or major) defeats and victories, toward the ongoing and ever-expanding triumph of God in history. God buries his workers but His work goes on.

Elijah had to realize that his ministry was only an episode in a very long-running saga. It would be good if we too had the humility to admit the same. We are part of something that has continuity with the past and also perpetuity in the future. It will end in triumph and not tragedy, and it will be God and not Satan who has the last word.

Passing the baton

Since like Elijah we live in a time of transition, it is important that we learn to handle that transition well. You have probably watched television athletic competitions which include relay races. The key to success in such a race frequently lies in the handover of the baton to the team member who is to run the next leg of the race. It is all too easy to fumble or even to drop that baton. This metaphor highlights both the importance of team effort and also the vital necessity of a properly executed handover if the race is to be won. Elijah nearly flunked on both counts. He forgot he was only a part of the team, and that there were other runners also in the race. (He miscalculated the number of his teammates by 6,999.) Worse still, he nearly dropped the baton. God reminded him that there were other people waiting for their chance to run, and more particularly, that Elijah had a successor waiting a few miles ahead of him round a bend in the track—Elisha. Elijah was to pass on the baton of his witness. His job was to make sure that he made the pass as smoothly and efficiently as possible.

We too live with the legacy of the past, we have a job to do now in the present, and we must also look expectantly to the future. You are to act like Elisha as you grasp the baton handed to you from the past, and as you prepare to hand that same baton to your successors. There are no stars in a relay race, unless it is the whole team of winners, in which case everyone is a star. We may be proud to be in the race at all, but we should be humble about our own particular part within it. Church history didn't begin in 1967 when I was converted, nor will it end at next summer's Bible Week or convention. In the great sweep we call history, God has already determined the glorious outcome. But it is a team effort: it doesn't depend entirely upon you or upon me. We are all to play our part, but it is *only* a part and not the whole.

However, each one of us has something unique to contribute. Elisha, the God-appointed successor of Elijah, did not have the same task or ministry as Elijah. God does something new in each generation. That is why it is not healthy for us to live in the past. We may study history and learn from it, but never live in it. There is no better time for me to be alive than now, and no better place for me to be living than right here, for being alive in this time and this place is God's will for me.

What's in a name?

We see that demonstrated clearly here with Elijah and Elisha. Elijah's name means "God is Yahweh." He was called to affirm that fact within a climate of relativism ("there is no such thing as absolute truth"), pluralism ("all religious insights are equally valid"), and syncretism ("all roads lead to God, so why not amalgamate their complementary perspectives?"). A time, in other words, not dissimilar to our own. Elijah lived to declare that Yahweh is God and that *only* Yahweh is God—not Ahab and his consort Jezebel, nor the Canaanite deity Baal and his consort Asherah—*only* Yahweh is God and both tribal kings and tribal deities are accountable to him. This is why Elijah's ministry was marked by confrontation and judgment. There were power encounters of devastating effectiveness including blistering drought and rock-splitting storms—all in order to establish the identity of the Being who really ruled the heavens. Was it Baal or was it Yahweh? Elijah lived up to his name. He established the fact that Yahweh is God. A similar calling rests upon God's prophetic people today. We too live in a time of rampant relativism, pluralism, syncretism, lies, and deception. Is nature our god, or is God the God of nature? Is

ecological ruin the worst reckoning mankind can face, or is eschatological ruin a far more certain and fearful prospect? God's people
are called to an Elijah ministry of prevailing prayer and powerful
preaching to unmask mankind's deceptions today.

Yet we are called to demonstrate not only the fact that God *is,*
but also the fact that God *saves.* The name Elisha means "God
saves." The church's task is not only to show the world who God is
(Elijah), but also that God saves (Elisha). This is the baton we
must run with in this generation. We need not only the role of
Elijah, but also that of Elisha. This being the case, it is time God's
Elisha heard God's call. Are you listening?

I'LL GIVE YOU A CALL SOMETIME

2

1 Kings 19:15-21

The call to confrontation

In the exciting record of the early church in the book of Acts, various "show-downs" punctuate the narrative at significant intervals. Peter and John don't mince words with a skeptical Jewish Council as they assert the true source of their power to heal a cripple and the unique place of importance God has given to Jesus: "Salvation is found in no one else, for there is no other name under heaven given to men by which we must be saved" (Acts 4:12). Later, those same apostles refuse the Council's restriction order on their preaching with the curt response, "We must obey God rather than men!" (Acts 5:29). Another cameo shows us Peter dealing with Simon the Sorcerer after the latter had attempted to infiltrate the Christian community hoping to buy into a piece of Peter's supernatural action. "May you and your money die together if you dare to think you can buy God's gifts with money! You'll never be part of all that God is doing by striking bargains and offering bribes. You're a crook! You're bent!" (see Acts 8:20-22). Later still, Paul meets resistance from the court magician Elymas as he attempts to convert the Roman governor on the island of Cyprus. Paul turns on Elymas with a look that could burn a hole through a steel door and says, in effect "You bag of wind and stooge of the devil, you are always picking fights with what is right! Well, this time you've bitten off more than you can chew—you've taken on God Himself! The game is up! I'm going to punch your lights out and you will be blind for a long stretch. You'll stumble around in a physical darkness to match the spiritual darkness you choose to live in. Then you can decide who's really a son of Jesus, you who call yourself 'Jesus' son' '(Bar Jesus)' "(Acts 13:10-11, my paraphrase).

It's obvious, isn't it? God gives his people power to confront evil with a verbal energy and spiritual strength sufficient to establish that it is God who really calls the shots in this world. This is the Elijah ministry we spoke of in the previous chapter. God calls us to witness to His reality and being. In that capacity as witnesses, we have the backing of heaven to do some very amazing things. This is how Revelation puts it:

> And I will give power to my two witnesses, and
> they will prophesy for 1,260 days, clothed in sack-
> cloth . . . If anyone tries to harm them, fire comes
> from their mouths and devours their enemies. This
> is how anyone who wants to harm them must die.
> These men have power to shut up the sky so that
> it will not rain during the time they are prophesy-
> ing; and they have power to turn the waters into
> blood and to strike the earth with every kind of
> plague as often as they want (Rev. 11:3-6).

Just like a Moses or an Elijah in their ancient conflicts with evil individuals, evil institutions, and evil religions, God's church has a similar arsenal of weaponry to use in her conflict with the forces that resist her witness to truth today. We are not called to be minor irritants to a world hostile both to God and to our message. We are called to assault evil and imprecate God's judgment upon it at those special times when God "fills us with the Spirit" and "gives us the power" to do so (cf. Acts 13:9 and Rev. 11:6).

The call to compassion

But our calling is not only to be God's Elijah, we also have a vocation to be God's Elisha, to show that "God saves." The question is, will we live up to that name? In order to demonstrate that truth we must hear God naming us, summoning us, and claiming us, and we must respond to his call. Naming is a powerful activity in the Bible. Whatever God names us we are authorized to do. The Scriptures teem with names and titles for the people of God: "The Household of God," the "Royal Priesthood," the "Light of the World," the "Salt of the Earth," the "Bride," the "Body of Christ," the "Temple of God." All of these carry significant meaning in connection with our status and function, living as we do in a hostile world, and authorized by God to represent both His name and His kingdom in that world. The church is the embassy of heaven in a hostile, God-resistant, and enemy-occupied environment.

We are examining the life of Elisha to see the characteristics which the prophet displayed in his capacity as God's chosen and anointed servant. His calling was not only to show the world that God is, but also to show the world what God is like; His character, His mercy, and what He longs to do for men and women in need.

Elijah had faced his challenges with commendable faithfulness and zeal, but now Elisha must face his own. He entered the same world: the same occult darkness was working behind the throne, the same twisted power of the state was imposing idolatry upon the nation, and the same cowardly compromise was the chief characteristic of so many of God's people. Elisha's world was very much like our own, with arrogant world leaders flashing their military prowess and might, resurgent occultism with its mass appeal and excitement, false religion creeping into the church and scores of once faithful groups capitulating to the fads and philosophies of men rather than choosing to remain loyal to God's revealed truth.

Elisha had a very demanding role to play in this environment, and needed all the clout he could muster in order to do that job effectively. This is why God commissioned Elijah to authorize Elisha to take on this assignment.

> The Lord said to him, "Go back the way you came, and go to the Desert of Damascus. When you get there, anoint Hazael king over Aram. Also, anoint Jehu son of Nimshi king over Israel, and anoint Elisha son of Shaphat from Abel Meholah to succeed you as prophet. . . . Yet I reserve seven thousand in Israel—all whose knees have not bowed down to Baal and all whose mouths have not kissed him."
>
> So Elijah went from there and found Elisha son of Shaphat. He was plowing with twelve yoke of oxen, and he himself was driving the twelfth pair. Elijah went up to him and threw his cloak around him. Elisha then left his oxen and ran after Elijah. "Let me kiss my father and mother goodby," he said, "and then I will come with you."
>
> "Go back," Elijah replied. "What have I done to you?"
>
> So Elisha left him and went back. He took his yoke of oxen and slaughtered them. He burned the plowing equipment to cook the meat and gave it to the people, and they ate. Then he set out to follow Elijah and became his attendant (1 Kings 19:15-16, 18-21).

God wants us to see what Elijah and Elisha saw, namely that God runs history. He had seven thousand people who had not bowed the knee to Baal. He has His people everywhere. They are waiting in the wings for their cue to play their scripted part for

Him in the drama we call history. It won't be easy to play this part. That is why we need to hear a call from God, for only a genuine call will sustain you in difficult times. We all have a calling of some kind awaiting us. You may not have discovered yours yet, but it is there. You cannot be *reconciled* to God without being *recruited* into His service, so if you are truly a son of God you also have the privilege of being His servant.

Hearing God's call

What is your calling? In broad terms it is to live like Elisha. He was called to speak and to live prophetically, to move powerfully, to minister to the needs of others effectively, to act fearlessly, to serve outsiders mercifully, and then to die gloriously. And even that was not the end of his ministry.

You are one of God's hidden servants. Like those seven thousand you may feel as if you've hidden in a cave for a long time up to now, or like Elisha you may have spent your whole life helping Dad on the farm. Whatever your life is now, God has more for you to do. God calls us to be teachers, writers, town planners, designers of software, nurses, secretaries, economists, and soldiers—the options are endless. However, the important questions are these: Are you sure you are God's man or God's woman in that situation? Are you acting as though you are?

Only the knowledge of God's call can help you to answer these questions in the affirmative. Some people have found it helpful to answer four simple inquiries as they've sought to discover their calling from God.

1. What do you feel prompted to do?

This may well be a constraint or pressure of the Holy Spirit upon your spirit. Sometimes it is no more than an idea or an interest; at other times it becomes an overwhelming burden you cannot escape.

Some of us who have a call to preach God's Word know what this feels like. A constraint came upon us, and built up to great intensity. It overcame our excuses and arguments until we could do nothing else but take active steps in order to answer that call. You'll feel something of the same cluster of emotions as God points you in the direction of your calling.

2. What do you feel pleasure in doing?

Surprise, surprise! God's call tallies with what you like doing anyway. Of course you may have to overcome your initial shock (Moses, Jeremiah, and Saul of Tarsus did), but once you start thinking about it or doing it, you find that you've never felt more alive, more fulfilled, or more happy. Your call does not bring you face-to-face with your worst nightmare, but allows you to walk into your most fantastic daydream. When God Himself has caused you to dream, then one day your dreams will come true and your vision will become a reality.

3. What do you feel power in doing?

The element of enablement or anointing comes at this point. Your ability is evident in those activities to which you have been called. "We have different gifts, according to the grace given us" (Rom. 12:6), as Paul expressed it. You will feel an energy in what you do if God has really authorized you to do it. The Holy Spirit's power will be upon you to equip you to perform this task.

4. What do you receive praise in doing?

People who know you well and who benefit from your gifting will repeatedly affirm you in it. This will confirm objectively the subjective leadings which you have already experienced, and your gifts will receive some kind of formal or informal recognition. Very frequently God's mandate is mediated through a human agent.

These are the main factors which are present in any genuine

call of God, and these factors were all present in Elisha's call. His unhesitating response to Elijah's actions indicates that he aspired to the prophetic role long before his encounter with Elijah. There was no hesitation; this was something he wanted to do. The subsequent narrative demonstrates clearly both his anointing of God and his approval by men.

Who, me?—the surprising grace of God

There are a few more elements worth noting in this brief narrative of Elisha's call. Elisha was going about his regular business: "He was plowing with twelve yoke of oxen" along with eleven of the farm hands presumably, since "he was driving the twelfth pair" (1 Kings 19:19). Without warning Elijah suddenly approached and threw his cloak around him.

The element of sovereignty
Neither Elijah nor Elisha initiated this—God did. The call was radical and uncompromising. Elisha felt claimed by God and there could be no bargaining or resisting. God is not looking for volunteers, He is looking for conscripts. The times are too tough for people who "fancy a go at that." We need men and women who have been chosen by God: the divine constraint must be there. Elijah was saying in effect, "Leave all and follow me. . . . You're God's chosen successor to me."

When this occurs it creates in our minds the clear impression that we have little option. Isn't this how James and John must have felt when they left their father's fishing business to follow Jesus? Isn't this how Levi felt when he resigned his post as a public tax official in order to align his life with Jesus (Luke. 5: 9-11, 27-28)? To hear God's call is like the touch of God on a man or woman's shoulder. It will catch us off guard.

The element of surprise

God's sovereign choice is usually a strange one, not least to those so chosen. The apostle Paul pricked the inflated balloon of Corinthian pride and elitism with these pointed words:

> Brothers, think of what you were when you were called. Not many of you were wise by human standards; not many were influential; not many were of noble birth. But God chose the foolish things of the world to shame the wise; God chose the weak things of the world to shame the strong. He chose the lowly things of this world and the despised things—and the things that are not—to nullify the things that are, so that no one may boast before him (1 Cor. 1:26-29).

God has bypassed the wise, the well-educated, articulate, and sophisticated. He has overlooked the mighty, the inherently powerful with their dominant personalities and felt "presence." He has skipped over the noble, the well-bred with their distinguished ancestry and aristocratic bearing.

Instead, God hand-picks the ignorant, the helpless, the lost, the last, the least, and the lowest. There are exceptions of course. It was Selina, Countess of Huntingdon, who pointed out that Paul said, "Not *many* noble;" he did not say "Not *any*." Elisha appears to have been relatively wealthy, coming from a farming background sufficiently profitable to have built up a capital of at least twenty-four oxen (that's equivalent to two or three Massey Ferguson tractors!) and around a dozen laborers. But the element of surprise is still there. It is amazing that out of seven thousand still faithful in Israel, God should have picked Elisha to be Elijah's successor; surprising most of all to Elisha himself. An old Puritan put it like this, "God seeth not as men seeth, neither doth he choose men because they are fit, but he fits men because he hath chosen them."

The element of surrender

Elisha didn't volunteer: it was God's idea. But that fact, sovereign and surprising as it is, does not negate the importance of human response. Elijah walked on ahead, giving Elisha time and space to respond. Elisha had been surprised by God's sovereignty; now it was a time for decision. He did not find this easy. He wanted to say good-bye to his parents first, but Elijah said, "Go back . . . what have I done to you?" (1 Kings 19:20).

Elijah was saying, "This is between you and God, Elisha. I'm not dragging or coercing you into my service. God is calling you into His. You will have to make your own decision whether or not you will follow this call. There will be danger, threats upon your life, criticism, disappointment. Blessings, of course . . . but it's up to you whether you are willing to pay the price in order to see those blessings."

Of course Elisha made the right decision. F. W. Boreham said, "We make our decisions and then our decisions turn round and make us." Things would never be the same again. In slaughtering his oxen, Elisha gave up his former career, his inheritance, and his financial security. In burning the plowing equipment, Elisha burned his bridges too. There could be no going back. This is a generation of Christians who want gains without pains. We are interested in short-term commitments, hoping that our former employer will keep our post at the firm open until we've done our stint for God. It is not possible! Hudson Taylor, the pioneer missionary to China, said, "God is looking for wicks to burn, the oil and the fire come free." Will you become one of those wicks? Are you prepared to "burn on" for God until He decides you have burned long enough and you "burn out?"

We have to make ourselves wholly available. Yet this is not the miserable option it might at first seem to be, for Elisha is next seen organizing a huge open-air barbecue with roast oxen on the menu, broiled over a pit of charcoal from the fire made by the burning plow-share. There is tremendous festivity and joy in sacrifice.

"Sacrifice is the ecstasy of giving the best we have to the one we love the most." We don't do God a favor by choosing His service, He did *us* the favor by choosing us for that service. Really get hold of that and you'll be launched into your career not only with joy but with T-bone steaks too!

At first this ministry was nothing spectacular. "Then he set out to follow Elijah and became his attendant" (v 21). God did not choose you to be a sensation but simply to be a servant. In God's kingdom the way up is down. If you want to exercise authority then you must first submit to it. It follows, then, that if "authority" is something of a "dirty word" to you, then you are not likely to impact your generation as Elisha did his. If you submit, you'll serve. If you serve, then one day you will also rule.

Elijah was resolved not to take his secrets down with him to the grave; they were to be passed on to another. But they could be passed on only to the kind of person who could be trusted with such power. What is such a person like? The simple answer is a humble person—a servant. Servants are people who will take on all kinds of roles and responsibilities which at first glance do not seem related to the "ministry" God has commissioned them to undertake. Servants just get on with what needs doing next.

Servants are people who know how to set up the chairs, lock up the building, mow the grass when someone is sick, care for the children while others are at a conference, send a bunch of flowers when they are needed most, arrange the refreshments, carry the bags, book the tickets, and live in the shadow of the man of God. God takes His time maturing His ministers, sometimes many years. It may seem an interminable period in which all you do is perform an endless sequence of thankless and unspectacular tasks.

And so, in the intervening years all God says is, "Serve. Help the man of God. Help him fulfill his vision. One day you'll get to fulfill yours, but not yet. In the meantime, this is My word to you—serve." And Elisha was evidently good at this. He became known as the one "who used to pour water on the hands of Elijah"

(2 Kings 3:11). That was all he was known for. He had no prayer letters or prayer partners, no one interviewed him in *Christianity Today*, he wrote no paperbacks and conducted no seminars. He wasn't on the international conference circuit. He just had a reputation for fetching water and pouring it over Elijah's hands. He had the reputation for being a wonderful servant.

It's not a bad reputation—in fact, if God calls you, it's the only reputation worth having.

Are you called?

3 BE PREPARED

1 Kings 19:19; 2 Kings 2:1-18

Wait for it!

Foreign tourists in Britain are said to be amazed by the amount of time we are prepared to spend in that great British institution—the queue. But this must not be mistaken for patience. It is not *patient* queuing. We do endure the wait in silence, true enough, but it should be known that we are not enjoying the experience; we are secretly frustrated with the delay. Most of us resent wasting our time. If the truth came out, the fact is that we hate being made to wait for anything.

Think about it. Nine months is a long time to wait for a couple who are expecting the birth of their first child. Or take those engaged students whose wedding may have been planned for after their graduation: a year is a very long time for people who are in love. The examples are endless—apprenticeships, training programs, internships—they all test our patience, our ability to endure, our commitment to the goal, and the genuineness of our call as we wait for the desired end.

There is probably no wait so testing as the wait we endure between the onset of a genuine call from God and its actual implementation in active ministry. There are occasions when the Lord seems to be really taking his time. The reason for this is simple. During that time gap, God is preparing us for what He has in mind for us to do. It is easy to underestimate the importance of preparation for ministry: we think we will step full-grown into that work. This is never so, for it takes time for us to be made ready. It can take years to shape our personality and giftings to fulfill the role God has for our lives; years in which we foolishly moan, whine, complain, and resist God's dealings with us.

The chronology of the narrative of the Bible in the two books of Kings suggests that it took around ten years from the incident when Elijah threw his cloak over the surprised shoulders of Elisha, and the next episode recorded for us here in 2 Kings 2:1-18. How long might it take for you? If you think in terms of multiples of ten years, you'll be pretty close to the mark; anything less is a bonus. Moses was forty years old when the stirrings began in his heart to act as the liberator of his fellow Hebrews in Egyptian slavery. His rash attempts to begin that ministry by slaying an Egyptian taskmaster were decidedly premature. It resulted in flight and escape, with another forty years yet to elapse while Moses worked in obscurity as a shepherd in the wilderness of the Sinai peninsula before his call was reiterated at the burning bush (Ex. 3:1-2). Saul of Tarsus was called to be an apostle to the Gentiles at his first encounter with the risen Lord on the Damascus road (see Acts 9:1-6; 26:15-18). He began his preaching ministry almost immediately, but most scholars agree that he was to spend the next ten years building a fine work in Antioch, alongside Barnabas, before the famous incident in Acts 13:1-2 when both men were sent for the first time on their apostolic mission. God takes time to prepare us.

While this preparation goes on, we must learn to trust God. God is in charge of our promotion. When it comes it will neither be too late, nor too early. Like all God's dealings it will be right on time. Preparation for that time is a complex process. All kinds of factors are brought to bear upon our lives. Unlabelled experiences and mystery packages come into our lives and they are unraveled very slowly. It is usually only after the event that we see what each particular episode was designed to accomplish. Each one was a testing, and then suddenly all the testing is over and we are released into the ministry we thought we should have commenced years before.

This is a clearly discernible pattern in Elisha's life, and today as Christians with a similar calling to "show the world that God saves" it is likely that God will prepare us for our launch in parallel ways.

Our preparation for ministry

The narrative here gives us a potpourri of various testing which came into Elisha's life just prior to his own launch into public ministry. These were probably typical of many incidents during the previous ten years. Many times, however, we go through our severest trials just before a major breakthrough. The darkest time is just before the dawn. There are four tests worth noting here.

1. The test of loyalty

There are three exchanges recorded in verses 2, 4, and 6 between Elijah and Elisha:

> Elijah said to Elisha, "Stay here; the Lord has sent me to Bethel.'
>
> But Elisha said, "As surely as the Lord lives and as you live, I will not leave you." So they went down to Bethel . . . . Then Elijah said to him, "Stay here, Elisha; the LORD has sent me to Jericho." And he replied, "As surely as the Lord lives and as you live, I will not leave you." So they went to Jericho . . . Then Elijah said to him, "Stay here; the LORD

has sent me to the Jordan."

And he replied, "As surely as the LORD lives and as you live, I will not leave you." So the two of them walked on (2 Kings 2:2, 4, 6).

The common element in these three exchanges is the order "Stay here," which came as a kind of command from Elijah's lips. Maybe Elijah wanted privacy. Did he know he was about to leave the earth and wished to spare Elisha some pain or distress at that sudden snatching and departure? This is possible, but it is more likely that it was a disguised test for Elisha's resolve, love for, and attachment to his master. In a similar way your loyalty will also be tested. No fewer than three times Elisha vowed his utter commitment.

We live in an age of rank fickleness and fragile commitments. People break even the most solemn engagements very lightly indeed. Obligations are loosely held and *convenient* love ("as long as it suits me") rather than *covenant* love ("whether I feel like it or not") marks what ought to be the most binding relationships like friendship, business, and marriage. This factor of brittle promises even affects relationships within the church.

There are lots of reasons for this. Our emotions swing violently and it is a common experience that our initial enthusiasm for this cause or these people soon wanes. We cool off, and conclude that this justifies total withdrawal from the situation. The involvement may have become routine or even boring. A Christian life which is a succession of thrills and exciting challenges looks more fun. Or perhaps more attractive options may present themselves—another job, another partner, another leader, another church. It's easier to face the embarrassment of leaving than to stay and face the pain of unresolved issues. It is far more difficult to see changes through or to ride the storms and to wait for better days.

Some people even spiritualize their unfaithfulness, "The Lord told me to leave . . . I had a prophecy to indicate that I should

change churches . . . God has removed my burden for this place . . ."
This may be the voice of God in some cases. Mostly, however, it
simply amounts to, "I just feel like going! I'm through with all this!
I'm out of here!"

For Elisha, leaving was not an option. Two things tied him: his
fear of God ("As surely as the Lord lives . . .") and his heart tie to
Elijah ("and as you live, I will not leave you"). These factors firmed
up the resolve of his will which was voiced repeatedly in his statements "I will not leave you . . . I will not leave you . . . I will not
leave you." It is a healthy thing in a marriage when divorce is not
an option. It is a healthy thing in any spiritual relationship (trainer
to disciple, leaders to people) when "divorce" is also not an option.

Throughout the Bible outstanding spiritual leaders struggled
with the pain of desertion. We sense the pain in Paul's words,
"Demas . . . has deserted me" (2 Tim. 4:10). Demas had been
seduced by the pull of the world, " . . . because he loved this world."
The pull of temporal gains had eroded his loyalty, and so he left his
Christian work and his association with the great Apostle Paul.

Loyalty is a decision of the will. Are you loyal in your friendships,
loyal to your marriage, loyal in your place of work, and loyal to your
church and its leaders? When the testing comes and you hear those
siren voices, "You'd be much happier with her . . . they don't love you
any more . . . you're not important around here . . . they'd love to get
rid of you," God is allowing your loyalty to be tested. Pass the test and
God will have many wonderful things in store for you.

2. The test of loneliness

> The company of the prophets at Bethel came out
> to Elisha and asked, "Do you know that the
> LORD is going to take your master from you
> today?"
>
> "Yes, I know," Elisha replied, "but do not speak
> of it."

Then Elijah said to him, "Stay here, Elisha; the LORD has sent me to Jericho." And he replied, "As surely as the LORD lives and as you live, I will not leave you." So they went to Jericho.

The company of the prophets at Jericho went up to Elisha and asked him, "Do you know that the LORD is going to take your master from you today?"

"Yes, I know," he replied, "but do not speak of it" (2 Kings 2:3-5).

There is a correct and healthy emphasis today upon teamwork and relationships within the service of God. We do need each other, and we therefore must work hard at both building those relationships and remaining loyal to them. Yet ministry can also be a very lonely calling. We may be shunned or criticized or misunderstood. Seasons of painful isolation can come on account of our faithfulness to God. We must be prepared for this, ready to stand apart and to be misunderstood. If you walk on ahead with a great dream then you have to be prepared to walk alone at times, until others have seen what you see and are prepared to walk where you walk.

Elisha met regularly with the students from the "school of the prophets", or the Bible college at Bethel, and also with those from its southern campus at Jericho. I hope I'm not doing them an injustice if I suggest three factors which isolated Elisha from them. The first was a hint of jealousy. The repetition of the phrase "Do you know that the Lord is going to take your master from you today?" sounds a little like gloating. Were they glad that a relationship they had seen but never shared was soon to be over and that a rift was soon to come in a ten-year partnership? People do envy what they perceive to be our advantages, our connections, and our privileges, and they may be secretly glad when we lose them. We feel vulnerable when our brothers gloat over our misfortune.

Second, it is possible Elisha was stung by the patronizing tone of these words. The prophets seemed to imply that Elisha's greatness would be shrunk to size when he no longer lived under Elijah's shadow. It was a big test of his security in his own identity. No longer linked with Elijah, would Elisha simply disappear from the scene, or would he emerge with a significant contribution of his own?

Third, this laid upon Elisha a great sense of responsibility. "The Lord is going to take your master from you today" must have brought home to Elisha that he was truly on his own. A great new burden was laid upon his shoulders. People were now looking to him as they had once looked to Elijah. The prophets were saying, "Can we expect a lead from you? Are you up to the task? Where do we go from here?" Elisha now knew that within hours he would be in charge, responsible to hear from God for himself, responsible to give a decisive lead to prophets and people, responsible to speak to God in a situation of danger and jeopardy; a situation where he could no longer say, "I wonder what Elijah will do. . . . Whew! I'm glad I'm not in his shoes."

A position of responsibility is a lonely place to be. However, if you are truly ordained for your position by God, then you must be prepared to face this kind of loneliness—the loneliness of envious colleagues, patronizing comments, and fearful responsibility.

3. The test of faith

> Fifty men of the company of the prophets went and stood at a distance, facing the place where Elijah and Elisha had stopped at the Jordan. Elijah took his cloak, rolled it up and struck the water with it. The water divided to the right and to the left, and the two of them crossed over on dry ground (2 Kings 2:7-8).

Biblical religion is unashamedly supernatural. We believe in a

God who intervenes directly in our world. Unlike the Deists of the eighteenth-century "Enlightenment," we do not believe that God is a cosmic clockmaker who wound up the mainspring of this universe and then went to bed early, leaving His cosmos to run itself in a manner as orderly and predictable as clockwork. The so-called "laws of science" may well be the pattern of God's familiar operations observable in His world, but God is free to interrupt, interact, and suspend those operations at any time. Indeed He frequently does so, and He often uses His people as instruments to convey those bursts of supernatural power. God's servants must learn to make themselves available to God to be used in these supernatural ways.

God is a liberator and the cardinal element in every miracle is that it is an act of liberation. This is why Elisha's first engagement with the supernatural is reminiscent of the Exodus. It was to remind him of Moses at the Red Sea. Elijah and Elisha were both liberators. They were called to defy oppressive rulers and to deliver oppressed people. This is our calling too. For this we need a faith that can get in touch with the power of the Spirit and make us a channel for that power to enter the world of ordinary experience. I suggest this is a simple definition of what it means to be "charismatic."[1]

If you desire an increase in your faith, then you must consent to having your faith tested. Our tendency, particularly in Western Christianity, is to domesticate God. We serve a tame God who would never shock or surprise anybody, least of all threaten our worldview or sense of security. Of course, even a superficial acquaintance with the Bible and the God of the Bible will assure us that this is not so. The picture presented in the Scriptures is of a God who is always on the move in His relentless war against evil. The trick for us is to learn to overcome our fears and to move with Him.

In his masterpiece, the children's classic fantasy *The Lion, the Witch and the Wardrobe,* C. S. Lewis has written a powerful allegory of Christ's war with Satan. The children, Peter, Edmund, Susan, and Lucy have entered Narnia, the magical land held in the icy grip of a usurper witch, the White Queen. The legitimate ruler, Aslan, is on the move to reconquer his kingdom. Mr. Beaver is explaining to the children who Aslan is.

> "I tell you he is the King of the wood and the son of the great Emperor-beyond-the-sea. Don't you know who is the King of Beasts? Aslan is a lion— the Lion, the great Lion.'
>
> 'Ooh!' said Susan, 'I'd thought he was a man. Is he—quite safe? I shall feel rather nervous about meeting a lion.'
>
> 'That you will, dearie, and no mistake,' said Mrs Beaver; 'if there's anyone who can appear before Aslan without their knees knocking, they're either braver than most or else just silly.'
>
> 'Then he isn't safe?' said Lucy.
>
> 'Safe?' said Mr Beaver; 'don't you hear what Mrs Beaver tells you? Who said anything about safe? 'Course he isn't safe. But he's good. He's the King, I tell you.'[2]

You and I need to become better acquainted with a God who is not predictable and more than a little scary, not safe—but good. Goodness and power are both made available to His people, to assist them in their proclamation and demonstration of the LORD's kingdom and its age-long fight against the usurper.

Elisha had to learn to walk closely with God and to exercise a faith which could tap the supernatural power of God. So do you. Note that while Elisha did this, the company of the prophets "stood at a distance," just as many of God's people throughout church history and in our own day distance themselves from active participation in these supernatural activities. But while they remain detached and aloof, Elisha sticks close to a man of God who knows how to move in that power. While fifty men from the theological seminary stand back, Elisha gets stuck in. He refuses to be merely a spectator, he wants to become a participant. He wants to become personally acquainted with the power of God.[3]

In order for this to happen, Elisha had to take some risks. Faith should probably be spelled RISK. Anyone who wants to grow in faith has to take some chances, take some risks. Here are some of the unpleasant consequences which Elisha risked.

The first risk was that of being shunned by his peers. How would the "company of the prophets" react from their safe distance? The greatest danger to the radical Christian who wants to move in power does not come from the "company of the skeptics"—the atheists, agnostics, and liberals. It comes from our fellow evangelicals, "the company of the prophets," who in some cases deny the Bible they profess to believe. The Jordan Elisha crossed was to be a dividing line to cut him off from the caution, love of the status quo, and mediocrity of others. He had to risk their disapproval. He risked becoming unpopular with his denomination, perhaps even being shunned by them as an "unbalanced extremist."

The second risk was that of falling into excess or danger. Hitting the river with his cloak was a strange thing to do. Headline: "Crazy Old Prophet Beats Jordan with Rolled-Up Cloak"—very embarrassing for Elisha. What if it had only partially worked? He could have gotten a good soaking or perhaps even drowned! In the Bible, the Jordan is symbolic as a place not only of separation but of death. This could have been the "death" of his reputation as a man of God. We have to risk that if we want to grow in faith for the supernatural.

The third risk was that of going out on a limb. The other side of Jordan was not safe. It was foreign territory, enemy-occupied, and dangerous. The supernatural sphere is not safe. Every healing is a foothold on Satan's dominion of disease and death. Every deliverance is a break-out from Satan's dungeons of demonization. Will you take some risks and go plunder some goods from strongholds Satan presently considers safely his own? Will you go out on a limb for God? Remember, it is always out on a limb that you gather the most fruit.

Of course, the river Jordan parted and they crossed over on dry ground. God honored His faith. Faith brings the unseen power of God into the seen realm of the world in which we live. Without faith it is impossible to please God (Heb. 11:6), and so if we are to become men and women of God who please God by getting His will done on earth, then we must become men and women of faith. You do not know what faith you have until it is tested, until another man of God says in effect, "Come with me, watch this ... now step out yourself." We live by faith or we do not live at all. Either we *venture* or we *vegetate*. Venturing is a risky business, but it is always a risk worth taking. Faith is daring to do something regardless of the consequences, because God has told you to do it.

4. The test of ambition

> When they had crossed, Elijah said to Elisha, "Tell me what can I do for you before I am taken from you?"
>
> "Let me inherit a double portion of your spirit," Elisha replied.
>
> "You have asked a difficult thing," Elijah said, "yet if you see me when I am taken from you, it will be yours—otherwise not" (2 Kings 2:9-10).

"What can I do for you before I am taken from you?" sounds as if Elijah was giving his younger associate a blank check. What would Elisha write in the box? What amount would he fill in? This is the test of ambition. Ambition is not a bad thing in itself—it is good. Ambition is the aspiration or hope we have for our own personal future and the future of the lives we are privileged to bless and take with us. Like hope itself, it is a form of faith in the future tense. The problem is that ambitions can be either spiritual or carnal in origin.

Carnal ambition would have prompted Elisha to ask for fame,

travel, financial security, and all the kudos that come with a tape ministry, top-selling Christian paperbacks, and top billing at a major international conference. Elisha asked for none of these. He did not want a "double portion" of Elijah's air-miles, salary, royalties, or tape sales—only a double portion of his spirit.

The "double portion" is the inheritance of the firstborn son in a Hebrew household when he comes to take on responsibilities as the head of the family upon the death of his father (Deut. 21:17). This shows that Elisha wanted to be regarded as Elijah's heir or successor. It also implies that Elisha had weighed the cost. He had seen that this job entailed the onerous responsibilities of confronting the royal family, challenging idolatry and demon worship, putting his life on the line, risking poverty and unpopularity. He did not want to be a sensation; he wanted to be a servant. He was putting first the kingdom of God and His righteousness. He wanted power to do what Elijah did.

In order to receive this "double portion," Elisha had to do three things. He had to keep *walking* with those who had it. "As they were walking along" (v 11a)—keep company with men and women of God who have the Spirit. Catch their heart. Read their biographies. Show up when they minister in it or conduct seminars about it. Power is imparted in these ways.

He had to keep *talking* with those who had it. "And talking together" (v 11b)—are you inquisitive? Ask around—find out some of the secrets of anointed servants of God.

He also had to keep *watching*. Elijah said, "If you see me when I am taken from you, it will be yours—otherwise not" (v 10). And sure enough, "Elisha saw this and cried out." Watch what others do. Imitate their ways. See the spectacular intervention of God in their lives and reach out for the same yourself. Develop perception, discernment, and sensitivity. One day you will see something you will never forget, and your life will never be the same again.

Elijah was a hard act to follow. Had Elisha secretly wished for Elijah's removal so that he could have star billing? I doubt it. Much more likely, Elisha had nervously awaited such a time feeling inadequate for the role and at times wondering how he'd got through the auditions and been earmarked for the part. At any rate, he felt inadequate and knew that he needed more power, more presence, and more "charisma."

And then, without warning, Elisha was ready. Circumstances changed rapidly, and he received his cue to step from the wings on to the center stage of God's history. His time had come. All those rehearsals, all those lines learned, all those actions practiced were now to pay off. Elijah left him in the most spectacular way, but he did not leave Elisha bereft, impoverished, and powerless. The "double portion" of his spirit came on Elisha.

At that moment Elisha violently tore off the clothes of a trainee and a servant. He shredded his old apprentice's uniform and picked up the cloak of a prophet. There could be no going back. There was a minor hitch, however. He was on the wrong side of the Jordan river with no boats, no bridges, no ferries, and no fords to help him cross over. No problem. He'd asked for a double portion of Elijah's power, and now came his opportunity to test it. In fact, he did the same ridiculous thing he'd seen Elijah do: he slapped the surface of the river with the second-hand cloak he'd just picked up. "Okay," he said defiantly, "where is the God of Elijah?" The implication was clear in the question, "If I'm really Elijah's successor and my time has really come, then what You did for him, do for me!" He didn't want the cloak for show but for action. He didn't want gifts to dangle as ornaments around his neck so he could show off with them. He wanted those gifts as tools to get the job done.

"Where is the God of Elijah?" Elijah may have gone, but Elijah's God is still here. That's what the company of the prophets recognized, "The spirit of Elijah is resting on Elisha" (v 15), but the question is, do you? Will you let God do through you today what He did through others in former days?

1. This definition is derived from Marcus J. Borg, *Jesus: A New Vision* (HarperSanFrancisco, 1987), p. 16.

2. C. S. Lewis, *The Lion, the Witch and the Wardrobe* (Puffin Books: 1959), p. 75.

3. Those needing help to reconsider their skeptical approach to the possibility of God's miraculous power working through his people today should read Jack Deere's clear, brilliantly argued and deeply moving case for miraculous gifts today. It is entitled *Surprised by the Power of the Spirit* (Kingsway: Eastbourne, 1994).

4 POLLUTION BUSTERS

2 Kings 2:19-25

Most informed people today share some measure of concern over the environmental damage we have done to the earth. The causes of the life-threatening trends and deadly effects upon our world are almost invariably analyzed in purely scientific, sociological, political, or economic terms. They are rarely, if ever, considered from a theological perspective.[1]

Now, while we have no brief to question the accuracy or integrity of the various secular analysts, it remains certain that the primary causes of these ecological disasters are both spiritual and moral. They are questions of a theological and ethical nature, so we must conclude that their primary solutions must also be theological and ethical. In short, the most serious pollution on planet Earth at this moment is the pollution of sin. Indeed, the primary cause of environmental pollution is also sin. Our ecological crisis is at root a *moral* crisis.

This is comparatively easy to demonstrate, even from the most cursory survey of the Bible. In Genesis the very origins of pain, disease, barrenness, unproductive conditions, entropy, and decay are all traced back to man's bid for autonomy and independence from his Creator (Gen. 3:14-19). The covenant nation of Israel was formed as a kind of dry run for God's ultimate intention of rescuing all mankind from the catastrophic effects of sin. Israel was given God's revealed law in order to shape and to guide the life and lifestyle of this new people. Yet even here, God warned of the consequences of further rebellion and apostasy in the strongest possible terms. He pronounced curses on the people if they were faithless; curses which would overtake both themselves and their environment. These are cataloged in Deuteronomy 28:16ff. They would affect city, country, crops, livestock, and land. Plague, disease, heat waves, and drought are all predicted, along with waves of physical, mental, emotional, and psychological distress.

The prophets who preached to the backslidden tribes of Israel between the eighth and sixth centuries B.C. reiterated these descriptions of the environmental effects of sin (see, for example, Amos 4:6-10, Isa. 24:4-7, Hosea 2:8-13, Joel 1:2-12, Jer. 12:10-13).

Not surprisingly, then, this emphatic connection between ethics and the environment, between man's pride and the earth's pollution, is also established by Jesus in His discourse on the signs of the end of the age recorded in Matthew 24. Jesus speaks in turn of the spiritual (v 4), social (v 6), international, and ecological (vv 7-8) effects of sin and unbelief upon the world in which we live. The same sequence of disasters is picked up in John's vision recorded in the book of Revelation.

There is a mandate resting upon the church of Jesus Christ to move out with the remedy to these disasters. It is significant that the long-term hope of the Old Testament prophets mentioned above included no less a prospect than the renovation of our polluted earth and its full recovery from the damage done to it by sinful men and women (e.g., Isa. 11:3-9; 65:17-25). Throughout the Scriptures God gives us hints of what will be fully revealed at the end of time. Jurgen Moltmann, professor of systematic theology in the University of Tubingen, says the righteousness of God is going to create a new world, and will be manifested only at the end of the time of this world, and in the daybreak of the new creation. Only then will the glory of the Lord appear. But even in the history of this world there are already revelations of the new world to come, revelations ahead of time. In the Old Testament, these revelations of God's future are linked with the callings of his prophets, and these calls are often founded on the vision of this coming divine glory (Isaiah 6).[2]

The fullest description of this new earth is saved for the very last disclosures given by special revelation and recorded by the apostle John in Revelation 21-22—a description which includes the statement "Nothing impure will ever enter it" (Rev. 21:27) and concludes with the reiterated imagery of Ezekiel (47:1-10) that the new world will have a clean river, abundant fruit, and a verdant leafy tree which will bring health to the people (Rev. 22:1-2). There will no longer be any curse because sin has finally been eliminated from God's creation.

This may seem far removed from our study of Elisha, but not so. Elisha's ministry opens with two remarkable incidents describing how he began to deploy the anointing of power which was now on his life. In a curious way, they draw our attention not only to the real problem, but also to the real solution.

Media information today draws attention away from the real problems, and rarely touches upon the real solutions. For example, the news features prominent reports of terrorist acts and inner-city violence. Statistically, however, your chances of being killed by a terrorist are 1 in 420,000. The chances of a homicidal attack in Norway are 1 in 100,000. Yet the chances of a baby being killed by abortion in the womb of a British woman are now 1 in 5, and in Rumania they are even higher at 1 in 1.6 pregnancies. This is supremely a spiritual problem. Spiritual problems need spiritual solutions and only truly spiritual people are capable of delivering them. This is where Elisha came in. This is where the church must come in too.

Elisha was the most influential figure of his day. He carried the spiritual cures for his nation's ills. The most significant people in the world today are Christian people. We too carry God's medicine for the diseases of the nations. God wants us to become involved, to move out with the power we have, to engage the real enemies around us, and to become "environmentally aware" in every sense of the word. It's not so much a case of becoming "green" as becoming "red hot" for God.

The two incidents which launched Elisha's ministry deal with environmental and moral pollution.

You can confront environmental pollution with God's blessing

> The men of the city said to Elisha, "Look, our lord, this town is well situated, as you can see, but the water is bad and the land is unproductive."
>
> "Bring me a new bowl," he said, "and put salt in it." So they brought it to him. Then he went out to the spring and threw the salt into it, saying, "This is what the LORD says: 'I have healed this water. Never again will it cause death or make the land unproductive.'" And the water has remained wholesome to this day, according to the word Elisha had spoken (2 Kings 2:19-22).

This book is not intended to be a "green" manifesto. My problem with "green" politics is not that they are too radical, but that they are not radical enough! To be "radical" means literally that we go to the root of issues. The roots of all human issues that we face

51

in this world are spiritual, and even those environmentally concerned individuals who do embrace "spiritual" perspectives generally embrace false ones. They are revised forms of paganism— worldviews which blur the distinction between the creature and the Creator, belief systems which end up either belittling or exaggerating the true worth of man. Man is seen either as a sod or a god, mere dirt or a deity, a chance conglomeration of molecules or an emanation of the universe, itself worthy of the worship which belongs to God alone. There is in this false spirituality an idolatry which transfers attention from the Creator to His creatures, and which like all idolatry, opens the lives of its participants to a trafficking with the demonic realm.

This is why neo-pagan thinking with its New Age optimism and legitimate concern for the earth is ultimately doomed to failure. It is out of line with reality, for it has no place for the God of the Bible. It is therefore most false where it needs to be most true. In every nation of the world facing ecological problems today, the root causes are connected with false religion.

False religion is man's bid to satisfy his longing for spiritual fulfillment independently from God. Since Adam we have always resented the fact that God sets boundaries to our existence and conditions to our freedom. We would rather botch up a self-made religion than submit to a divinely given revelation. God has given man the ability to rule, but it is a dominion with responsibility and accountability to the God who made us. Roy Clements comments astutely on the connection between spiritual causes and environmental effects:

> We rule but our dominion is a stewardship, limited by the sovereignty of the God who delegates it to us. So there has to be a 'but'. And the reason our world is in a mess is that we human beings resent the 'but'. We were not content with the humble dignity of being made in the image of God. In

arrogance we grasped at deity itself. We wanted no inhibiting 'buts' limiting our freedom of action. We wanted moral autonomy, we wanted to rule not only the world but ourselves. And there lies the root of our ecological crises. There is the source of our economic recessions. There is the source of all our frustrated longings for Utopia. We do not want to be commanded.

He also points out:

One of the things which Eastern religion does is to import a superstitious reverence for nature which inhibits our willingness to control our environment. Hinduism teaches that there are no ultimate distinctions in the universe; everything is a manifestation of one cosmic spirit; everything is divine. And the result of that, of course, is that people go hungry rather than kill the rats or the cows that eat the corn. Science can never grow out of that pantheistic world view. From an Eastern mystical point of view, it would be essentially irreligious to name things. To distinguish yourself from other things and stand over against them, to objectify them and analyze them, is to deny the essential oneness of everything. According to Eastern religion, such science is unspiritual and impious.[3]

In order to have correct perspectives on how to solve some of the world's problems, we need correct perspectives upon the nature of the world itself. Certainly Christian believers are to be concerned about the environment. The promise of the renovation of the earth is a major dimension of Christian hope (Rev. 21:1, 5;

Acts 3:21; Matt. 19:28; Rom. 8:18ff and Isa. 65:17-18). As David Pawson points out, this is no pipe dream, for it has been guaranteed by the resurrection of Jesus Christ from the dead. Jesus" body was the first part of the old creation to be dissolved and recreated thus rendering inevitable the renovation of the rest. He comments,

> Such a hope is bound to affect the Christian attitude to this planet. The responsibility to be good stewards of the earth entrusted to us, husbanding its resources and protecting it from abuse and exploitation, is very clear in the Bible. . . . But the knowledge that this is not the only earth we shall ever have to live on prevents the despair or panic that can motivate the 'green' movement. This can be pursued with a religious fervor that is in danger of replacing Father God with 'Mother Earth' bordering on a revival of the fertility cults which were such a snare for ancient Israel. It is idolatry to become devoted to the creation rather than the Creator, it is to exchange the truth for a lie (Romans 1:25). In this case, the lie is that our future is in the hands of 'Mother' nature and that her future is in our hands. The truth is that our future and 'hers' are in God's hands.[4]

Elisha was still at Jericho, near the Dead Sea, about five miles west of the River Jordan. It is a hot, barren, and extremely hostile environment. I once visited the areas to walk the mound that marks the ruins of the ancient city once conquered by Joshua. A new town has developed nearby, and fresh waters flowing through the area have made it something of an oasis in the desert. Palms and sycamores sway with lush green foliage, and street vendors line the roadway selling huge quantities of the varied and luscious fruits grown in the immediate vicinity. But this was not always the case.

Clearly in Elisha's time some ecological problem had overtaken the city, and its citizens said, "This town is well situated, but the water is bad and the land is unproductive" (2 Kings 2:19).

Similarly, great civilizations and beautiful cities can hide rampant corruption. Magnificent cathedrals may be the cover for powerless religion. We have to learn to see beyond the surface of things. Jericho is a picture of this world. Behind the facade a polluted stream runs through it. The soil is toxic and the result is crop failure and low productivity. Hunger and want are the result.

Turning to the right man

The people of Jericho turned to the right man for help. We noticed earlier how the school of the prophets recognized the new anointing on Elisha: "The company of the prophets ... said, 'The spirit of Elijah is resting on Elisha' " (2 Kings 2:15). Elisha was therefore requested to do something about their problem.

When was the last time the church was asked to do anything by the world? Christians are regarded as fools, fakes, and charlatans. We are rarely consulted for our views on anything of importance, let alone the answers to the nations' ills. The common conception is that we are world-denying ascetics uninterested in the environment and universe God has created. This is a lie. Christians are world-affirming, not world-rejecting. But a day is coming when the anointing on God's church will be so great that people will turn to us with respect to ask us what we know and what we can do: "Look, our lord ... the water is bad and the land is unproductive." It's time the people of the world asked the people of God what God can do about the problems of the world.

The Old Testament is pervaded with promises concerning God's plans for the created world in which we live. Old Testament scholar William Dumbrell, commenting on the comprehensive covenant which God made with Noah, says that Genesis 9 makes it clear that the covenant with Noah had the preservation of the created order in view, but this in itself is a redemptive exercise on the widest scale. The restoration of man is bound to affect his world and consistently with this, the New Testament asserts strongly that the redemption of the creature must involve the redemption of creation.

God's plans clearly include His purposes both for mankind and the universe he inhabits. Dumbrell goes on:

The world and man are part of one total divine construct and we cannot entertain the salvation of man in isolation from the world which he has affected. The refusal to submit to Eden meant a disordered universe and thus the restoration of all things will put God, man, and the world at harmony again.[5]

The prophets reiterate God's long-term plans in the form of glowing promises. While we can acknowledge that many of these prophetic foreviews seem to be couched exclusively in terms of God's plans for ethnic Israel and her future in the Promised Land, Chris Wright is surely in line with the whole tenor of Scripture as it bears upon eschatological (end-time) issues when he says:

A foretaste of that new creation is seen in the otherwise extravagant language with which the prophets look forward to the renewal of the land of Israel itself (Jer. 31:10-14, Ezek. 34:26-29, 36:8-12). As elsewhere in the Bible, the land of Israel functions in part as a token of the future new creation, as the place of God's presence and unhin-dered blessing.[6]

If this accurately represents the essence of God's plans for His earth, then it carries implications for all the peoples of the earth—particularly those who suffer most from the fallout of sin, namely the poor who have a special place in the heart of God.

The time is long overdue for the poorer nations of the world to be able to turn to God's people for the answers to their poverty. It is time our own nation turned to Christians for answers to the enormous issues which are sapping the vitality of our people. Those answers do not lie in politics and legislation, because the answers are spiritual. The greatest causes of poverty and environmental and social decay are spiritual. When we look at Deuteronomy 28, we see that God curses a land with failure, humiliation, dry climate, physical and mental disease, family breakdown, terrorism, barrenness, plunder, and robbery. Why? Deuteronomy lists four simple causes:

1. The worship of false gods.
2. Disrespect for authority, particularly that of parents.
3. Lawlessness with its accompanying rebellious behavior.
4. All forms of illicit and unnatural sex, and rampant sensuality.

Only righteousness can exalt a nation. Sin is a reproach to any people. It is time the nation asked righteous people how it can be put right. If the people are put right then the environment itself will experience remedial treatment. I have never heard a spokesperson for "green" issues even touch on the above four roots of environmental pollution, have you?

Turning to the right solution

The men of Jericho didn't only come to the right person, they went away with the right answers. Elisha was a man who could make a difference. His very presence affected his environment. He was a *thermostat* rather than a *thermometer*—unlike so many believers who merely reflect conditions where they live and work, rather than reforming them. The presence of even ten believers in a city should have an incalculable effect—it would have saved the cities of Sodom and Gomorrah from destruction (see Gen. 18:32). Here we see what just *one* man could do.

In Elisha we see a beautiful combination of symbolic action and Spirit-given words. This is not simply a matter of throwing bowls of sea salt into polluted streams; it is a question of acting and speaking in ways which God Himself has authorized if we are to become more effective as Christians today. To be a Christian is to be a key person in the world situation today, but we have to make our presence felt. The American preacher Vance Havner once commented, "The same church members who'll yell like Commanche Indians at the football game on Saturday sit like wooden Indians in church on Sunday!" Yes, and frequently for the rest of the week too. It's not just Christians we need; it is Christians of the right kind. These effective agents of change will be marked by three features.

1. They will be clean vessels

"Bring me a *new* bowl" (v 20a). God wants his people set apart from common standards and common use. He wants us clean inside and out. Robert Murray McCheyne, a pastor who saw revival in his parish in Scotland during the early part of the last century, once said, "A holy minister is an awesome weapon in the hands of God." Too often our effectiveness is blunted due to the rusting defilement of the wrong kind of entanglements—often sexual ones. Paul wrote, ["For this is the will of God, your sanctification"] (i.e., your separation from the world so that you can be dedicated to the purposes of God) ["that you should abstain from sexual immorality, that each of you should know how to possess his own vessel in sanctification and honor, not in passion of lust like the Gentiles who do not know God"] (1 Thes. 4:3 NKJV). Statistically speaking, however, the incidence of sexual immorality among church members is almost as high as that among their unchurched counterparts. No wonder we have very little to say on these issues. There is something peculiarly defiling about sexual sin. "Flee from sexual immorality. All other sins a man commits are outside his body, but he who sins sexually sins against his own body" (1 Cor. 6:18). God is looking for a new breed of Christians, clean ones, to use as world-changers in these present crises.

2. They will have a salty influence

"And put salt in it." Salt was acquired in huge quantities from the shores of the nearby Dead Sea. Rapid evaporation in that hot climate left a 25 percent saline content in those waters, and unusual formations of deposited salts were accumulated on the shore. If this salt lay around unused, then over time, the effect of rain and sun on these salt deposits was to leech out the saline content leaving only a useless grit behind. Jesus spoke of "salt that has lost its saltiness" and which is fit for nothing (Luke 14:34). Many Christians are not only like salt that has lost its savor but pepper that has lost its pep! However, salt in good condition was used primarily for two purposes in the ancient world: as a preservative, to arrest corruption, and as an additive, to bring out the flavor in food and help with digestion. Salt destroys harmful bacteria and so slows down the processes of decay; it also helps digestion since salt is necessary to all animal life. Our bodies have an instinctive taste for salt in some form or other.

Elisha threw this salt into the place where it was most needed, the polluted stream, the source of Jericho's life, and that is exactly where Christians most need to be active—in the most influential sources of a nation's life. For us these spheres include schools and education, arts and entertainment, national and local government, finance and industry, sport and media, the trade unions and social services, our hospitals and other caring agencies. God wants us there to arrest corruption, to purify, and to bring a new flavor or quality to each of these activities.

If it wasn't for the church, Satan would already have turned earth into an outpost of hell. The fact that the world has been preserved from total devastation proves that many of God's people are functioning effectively in all of these realms.

3. They will speak with authority

Elisha performed the symbolic action but he also spoke the God-given word, "This is what the Lord says: 'I have healed this water. Never again will it cause death or make the land unproductive'" (v 21). Paul Billheimer said,

> Through the use of her weapons of prayer and faith she [the church] holds in this present throbbing moment the balance of power in world affairs. In spite of all her lamentable weaknesses, appalling failures and indefensible shortcomings the church is the mightiest force for civilization and enlightened social consciousness in the world today.[7]

God has indeed given His people authority. He holds us responsible to enforce His will and to administer His directives in the earth today. We are to catch God's mind and speak His thoughts as a *rhema* word—a specific word for a specific situation—from God to those around us. We do this by many means: we pray, we testify, we prophesy, we teach, we preach. Here we see Elisha prophetically speaking forth words—but not just any words. They are words of creative force, words that will effect change. He confronts, names, and calls a halt to corruption. He speaks wholeness into the situation. He commands fruitfulness from that point onwards to be the prevailing situation on into perpetuity. In this capacity, Elisha was acting as a forerunner of Jesus Himself.

Jesus came into the world to undo all the damage sin and Satan have done to God's universe. Jurgen Moltmann sums up the plight of the men and women to whom Jesus addresses his ministry: "His message is addressed to the poor, the wretched, the sick and the hopeless, because these are the people who suffer most from God's remoteness and human hostility." God's remoteness? Yes, God seems remote, but in Jesus God has come near, "the kingdom of heaven is at hand."

> This gives us a new angle from which to view the ministry of Jesus. When Jesus expels demons and heals the sick, he is driving out of creation the powers of destruction, and is healing and restoring created beings who are hurt and sick. Jesus" healings are not supernatural miracles in a natural world. They are the only truly "natural" thing in a world that is unnatural, demonized and wounded . . . . The gospel assures the poor of God's life-giving, newly creating activity. The gospel is realistic, not idealistic. It does not bring new teaching; it brings new reality. That is why what is most important for Jesus is his quarrel with poverty, sickness, demonism and forsakenness, not his quarrel with the teaching of the Pharisees and the Sadducees.[8]

In speaking over the polluted water in the way that he did, Elisha was demonstrating the power and authority which would arrive in its fullness centuries later in the ministry of Jesus Himself; the same power, in fact, which Jesus has in turn conferred upon His anointed people, the church.

Of course it is impossible by one action and a few words to produce a lasting effect on running water unless God is in that action and in those words. Yet although verse 22 was penned around 2,500 years ago, we can still say, "And the water has remained wholesome to this day." The spring at modern Jericho is still sweet, and it is still called "Elisha's Fountain." After all, it was "according to the word Elisha had spoken."

God loves to use you and me in similarly powerful ways. You are where you are today for the purpose of taking the poison, the barrenness, and the death out of your environment and transforming it into an oasis of interest, color, humor, sparkle and life—just as Elisha did.

You can confront moral pollution with God's curse

> From there Elisha went up to Bethel. As he was walking along the road, some youths came out of the town and jeered at him. "Go on up, you baldhead!" they said. "Go on up, you baldhead!" He turned around, looked at them and called down a curse on them in the name of the LORD. Then two bears came out of the woods and mauled forty-two of the youths. And he went on to Mount Carmel and from there returned to Samaria (2 Kings 2:23-25).

This incident followed immediately after the miracle of the purified water. It shows that advance is usually followed by counterattack; step forward and you risk being slapped back. People are either for God or against Him; that is why there is no such thing as spiritual neutrality. The pioneer missionary C. T. Studd said, "Be extravagant for God or for the Devil, but for God's sake don't be tepid."

True righteousness cuts, and it cuts both ways. It brings mercy and healing into the lives of people of good heart, but it also brings crisis and judgment to fools who mess around with it. Godliness is not necessarily to be equated with "niceness." You perhaps realize that the apostle Paul does not list "niceness" as a fruit of the Spirit in Galatians 5, and as a Spirit-filled man there were occasions when Paul was not very nice at all! (See for example Acts 14:9-12; Gal. 5:12.)

Of course this passage is a stumbling block to some! It offends their sensibilities to see men of God setting she-bears onto little boys just for having a little joke at their expense. Was Elisha a crusty old eccentric, over-sensitive, and more than a little insecure about his hair-loss problem? Possibly, but we need to say one or two things in his defense.

First, these were probably not "boys" as we would understand it. The Hebrew word translated "youths" could include young men of anything up to around thirty years of age. They were probably adults, and at any rate we have to conclude that they were fully responsible for their actions. In any rough city like Jericho, or Glasgow, Chicago, or Los Angeles, a gang of "youths" can be a frightening and very threatening force to encounter.

Second, this doesn't appear to have been a joke. This was a deliberate pursuit, a hounding of God's prophet designed both to insult and to intimidate him. In short, this was no laughing matter. This was a mark of deep irreverence, the mockery of true spiritual authority characteristic of all declining cultures even to our own day. As such it calls for the serious judgment of God.

These youths were showing a deep contempt for the supernatural power of God. They called out, "Go on up . . . go on up . . . you baldhead." This was possibly a reference to Elijah's unusual departure in the fiery chariot, so that they were not only expressing the wish to get rid of Elisha in a similar way, even before his ministry had barely started, they were putting God to the test: "Let's see that chariot for ourselves, go on, beam him up . . . send the heavenly taxi service . . . swing low, sweet chariot—coming for to take him home!" We see similar scorn around us today whenever God is powerfully at work. They showed contempt for age and maturity. Whether Elisha's baldness was shaved or natural we can't say for sure. But since balding is often a sign of aging and of failing powers, it is sometimes viewed contemptuously. All I can say is, be very careful what you say to balding men in the future!

Above all, they showed contempt for God's authority. These

young men had seen the water supply of Jericho cleaned up "according to the word Elisha had spoken." They saw God back up his prophet for the benefit of their people. They were clearly not very impressed. Some people aren't. That's why God says, "Do not touch my anointed ones; do my prophets no harm" (Ps. 105:15).

No sins are more serious than these. This was not a case of "boys will be boys," a few lads having a little harmless fun. This was spiritual rebellion and anarchy of the worst kind. It was overt wickedness, satanically inspired corruption and a demonic blasphemy akin to the blasphemy against the Holy Spirit. If this is what the youths of the town were like, what were conditions like in the city in the years leading up to Elisha's visit? Could this spiritual ignorance, irreverence, and unbelief have been the root cause of the environmental problems Elisha had so recently cured?

I believe so. And if I am right, then we must view with equal seriousness the mockery of the church, the Bible, Christian ministers, and Christian witness in our nation today. It is a mockery of God Himself. Where there is loss of respect for God's authority, then parents, teachers, government, and police have little chance of maintaining respect for themselves. If the foundations are crumbling, then the superstructure is set for a fall too.

That is why Elisha cursed it. "He called down a curse on them in the name of the Lord." A curse is when man or God speaks against you and invokes harm upon you as a judgment. Curses are powerful. When God speaks up for you no man can speak against you, but when God speaks out against you no man can speak up for you.

A curse is an anticipation in time of the judgment of God which will be meted out fully in eternity. Just as a blessing gives a man a taste of heaven on earth before he gets there, so a curse gives a man a taste of hell on earth before he gets there. A curse is a severe warning of the consequences of sin. They met a she-bear on earth so they wouldn't have to meet an angry God in eternity. I hope they took on board the lesson: better repent of mocking

God's prophet now so you won't have to regret being mocked by God Himself later.

Destined for the cutting-room floor

Movie censors sometimes cut scenes from films so that the public will not be offended. Can we take a similar approach to the Bible? After all, the Bible is full of "offensive" material, especially material concerned with the judgment of God upon sin. This material is there to teach us the danger of defying God. It's easier to defy the law of gravity than it is to defy God. You may as well run like a cat into the blades of a lawnmower as run contemptuously into the face of God's power and God's truth. You may as well head-butt a brick wall as butt in on God's prophets—try to stop them and God will stop you.

Elisha shows us that God has given His people power to curse sin and to remove it when necessary. God will use Christians either to change the hearts of the devil's agents or to remove those agents. In the former case we are then free to remove the symptoms—a polluted environment; in the latter we can remove the cause—a polluted people. Either way, we are here to make a difference. We are a dangerous people.

"Don't mess with praying people"—that's the thrust of this passage. S. D. Gordon said, "The greatest thing anyone can do for God or for man is to pray." It is not our role merely to lament terrorism, the rising tide of blasphemy, and the alarming expansion of anti-Christian religion—we are to pray against them. We can ask God to rebuke the demons who control them, and to curse the sin at work within them.

All heaven can break loose when God's prophetic people step out and speak out. Let's confront pollution for what it is—a manifestation of man's rebellion against his Creator. The remedy is the cleansing blood of Jesus and powerful anointing of His Holy Spirit.

1. For a highly readable yet solidly informed theological exploration of the environmental issues touched upon in this chapter, I recommend Lawrence Osborn, *Guardians of Creation* (Apollos Books, InterVarsity Press: Leicester, 1993).

2. Jurgen Moltmann, *The Way of Jesus Christ* (SCM: 1990), p. 219.

3. Roy Clements, *Masterplan—How God Makes Sense of Our World* (IVP: Leicester, 1994), pp. 31, 27.

4. David Pawson, *The Resurrection* (Sovereign World Ltd: Kent, England, 1993), p. 55. See also John R. W. Stott, *The Authentic Jesus* (Marshall Pickering: London, 1992), pp. 46-47.

5. William J. Dumbrell, *Covenant and Creation* (The Paternoster Press: Exeter, 1984), p. 41.

6. Chris Wright, *Knowing Jesus Through the Old Testament* (Marshall Pickering: London), pp. 100-101.

7. Paul E. Billheimer, *Destined for the Throne* (Christian Literature Crusade Inc: 1975), p. 16.

8. Jurgen Moltmann, *The Way of Jesus Christ* (SCM: London, 1990), pp. 96-99.

A TALE OF THREE KINGS

5

2 Kings 3

We are using these episodes which narrate the words and deeds of Elisha as a paradigm or model for the kind of role God is charging His people, the church, to exercise today. Our mission is to show the world that God saves. If we are to be fully engaged in that task there has to be a large-scale awakening on our part to the spiritual realities explicitly unfolded in God's Word. This awakening should stir us to recognize the kind of resources God has laid at our disposal, and the obligation upon us to deploy those resources to the maximum effect.

We now come to 2 Kings 3 with its story of the coalition of three strange bedfellows, namely, the kings of Israel, Judah, and Edom and their joint crusade against the king of Moab. It is a vivid portrait of God's people in compromise and weakness. At the same time, it shows how God brings us to a sense of clarity and direction and then uses us to overthrow the real enemy.

The coalition of the kings—spiritual compromise

King Joram of Israel, the northern kingdom, was a man who knew how to mobilize his people, stir them to action, and drum up support for an apparently noble cause. There seemed to be no shortage of troops ready to fight to guarantee the effectiveness of his mission. Other leaders affirmed their backing and he even had the sympathy of the leader of one of the world's great religions— the king of Moab. This is a picture of the church doing its best to get by without God; to fight for its cause without the divine word, without divine direction, and without divine power.

Man-made beliefs

> Joram son of Ahab became king of Israel in Samaria in the eighteenth year of Jehoshaphat king of Judah, and he reigned for twelve years. He did evil in the eyes of the Lord, but not as his father and mother had done. He got rid of the sacred stone of Baal that his father had made. Nevertheless he clung to the sins of Jeroboam son of Nebat, which he had caused Israel to commit; he did not turn away from them (2 Kings 3:1-3).

Joram is a vivid demonstration of the fact that it is impossible both to compromise with sin and to fight it effectively at the same time. Joram was the son of the notorious King Ahab, a king who had sponsored on a grand scale the state worship of Canaanite "nature" gods, Baal and Asherah, with their lewd sensualism and dark magic powers. The narrative is generous to him in that it tells us that Joram reacted righteously to the presence of this defiling worship. He "got rid of the sacred stone of Baal which his father had made" (v 2). Nevertheless, the spiritual foundations of the ten-tribe northern kingdom had been false from the start. Its founder Jeroboam, a former official in Solomon's court, had led a rebellion against Solomon's legitimate heir, Rehoboam, and won over all the embittered tribes of Israel except for Benjamin and Judah who remained true to Solomon's rightful successor (1 Kings 12).

Jeroboam was understandably nervous that the initial loyalty and enthusiasm of the ten tribes would not last for long while they had no access to the center of worship at the temple of Jerusalem. He therefore felt compelled to set up rival centers in his own territory at Bethel and Dan. He still couldn't hope to compete with the glories of Solomon's temple at Jerusalem unless he did something completely innovative, something exciting and new. The solution was to erect two golden calves as the focus and medium for the people's worship of Yahweh. The calf was a Canaanite fertility symbol. It was associated with the worship of those filthy sex-gods, Baal and Asherah. Jeroboam thus lapsed into religious syncretism. Syncretism is the attempt religious people sincerely make on a frequent basis, to meld together what they see as the best and most attractive features of two utterly incompatible systems of religious belief. This is dead wrong, for it elevates false gods to a place of importance, and worse still, it degrades God to a lower estimation in the minds of unthinking observers. Yahweh becomes like any other god, a competitor for the scarce attention of men.

Most New Age cults and activities today are syncretist. Freemasonry is syncretist. Hinduism is syncretist. Likewise, many popular cults which originated in the last hundred years or so—cults like Mormonism, Christian Science, Spiritualism, Theosophy and Hinduism-based movements like Transcendental Meditation, the guru Maharaj Ji, the Divine Light Mission, and Hare Krishna. Most people have also heard of the Korean religious leader the Reverend Sun Myung Moon and his Unification Church (The Holy Spirit Association for the Unification of World Christianity, Inc.), which is also syncretist in outlook.

Perhaps you can understand why that arch-syncretist Jeroboam has such a bad press in the Old Testament. A kingdom founded on spiritual compromise such as this was in desperate need of reformation. Yet Joram perpetuated this sin. He still believed that those two calves erected at Bethel and Dan could act as a pedestal for the presence of Yahweh—even though the simple people began to believe that Yahweh was a golden calf, who was impressed when his worshipers copulated at the foot of his pedestal.

The church today is rife with man-made attempts to stitch contemporary philosophy into biblical narratives; to make Jesus Christ a tribal deity brought out only on state occasions to formalize a royal wedding or opening of a stately affair; to confuse the invisible God with visible forms. The result is a double life led by worshipers at these syncretist shrines. People who are preoccupied with social cohesion, good feelings, and merely surface appearances rather than the true God will often tolerate hidden sin (particularly sexual sin) in their own lives and also the lives of others.

Man-made priorities

> Now Mesha king of Moab raised sheep, and he had to supply the king of Israel with a hundred thousand lambs and with the wool of a hundred thousand rams. But after Ahab died, the king of Moab rebelled against the king of Israel (2 Kings 3:4-5).

For 150 years the Moabites, a hostile nation to the east of the Dead Sea, had paid annual tribute to Israel of 100,000 lambs and 100,000 ram fleeces. When Ahab died, their current king, Mesha, saw this as a window of opportunity to assert his independence and stop paying this sizable annual sum of "protection money" to those "gangsters" northwest of his kingdom. Joram was decidedly put out! That was a lot of mutton and a great number of woolly rugs for the fireplace simply to write off as a "bad payer." He was very upset; upset enough to go to war.

Joram's primary concern was mammon, not the glory of God. His priority was the maintenance of material wealth and not the enhancement of God's glory. He was putting first the kingdom of man and its prosperity rather than the kingdom of God and its righteousness.

What about you? Does a rise in mortgage interest payments, a crash on the stock market, a scratch on the car, or the burglary of your video recorder arouse more passion in you than hearing Jesus' name used as an expletive, or the possibility that your church has seen no conversions for three months, or that your children are bored with church altogether and don't want to come anymore?

John Blanchard once put the issue like this, "It is perhaps the greatest sin of the greatest number of Christians, that in so many details of life they put God second."

Man-made alliances

> So at that time King Joram set out from Samaria and mobilized all Israel. He also sent this message to Jehoshaphat king of Judah: "The king of Moab has rebelled against me. Will you go with me to fight against Moab?"
>
> "I will go with you," he replied. "I am as you are, my people as your people, my horses as your horses" (2 Kings 3:6-7).

Joram concluded that "unity is strength." He was an ecumenist. He believed that people should get together. And so he embroiled the southern kingdom of Judah, in the person of its leader Jehoshaphat, in his fight. In addition, the king of a non-Israelite nation bordering upon Israel, Edom, was also roped in.

Frequently when men talk of "unity" they mean something altogether different from the Bible's understanding of true unity. What they mean is "union" or "unification"—humanly engineered and contrived alliances designed to further purely human goals based upon human compromise. That was surely the case here. When the Bible speaks of unity, however, it means something much more profound. It means unanimity, common agreement on the same beliefs and the same goals. Luke speaks of the early church in this way: "All the believers were one in heart and mind" (Acts 4:32), and Paul spoke of a unity which believers are called both to maintain: "Make every effort to keep the unity of the Spirit through the bond of peace," and attain "until we all reach unity in the faith and in the knowledge of the Son of God and become mature, attaining to the whole measure of the fullness of Christ" (Eph. 4:3, 13).

This is a far cry from Joram's flimsy amalgamation of confused and greedy monarchs on a crusade together simply to further their own ends. Yet this is an accurate caricature of many misguided attempts at "unity" in the church today. Gerald Coates summed up these efforts nicely in a very wry comment: "Placing two coffins side by side will not produce a resurrection." Unity cannot be organized where the participants are devoid of authentic spiritual life.

The best of the bunch was Jehoshaphat, but even he rallied to the wrong slogan. "We are the defenders of the free world!" said Joram (or something like it), and Jehoshaphat made an uneasy military alliance for purely political reasons; spiritual considerations never even entered into it. Jehoshaphat's sincerity is not in question. It was a noble gesture in that he sent a couple of aircraft carriers, hundreds of tanks, and personnel vehicles along with thousands of soldiers to help the war effort, but he never stopped to ask whether or not God was in this. And so their punitive strike against Moab was launched. Even one of the Arab nations joined in, perhaps out of jealousy or spite against Moab. Edom was keeping some strange company, and no one in Israel even paused to ask if this expedition had God's approval.

Some "unity" is not in the will of God. Unity is important, of course, but not at any price. Division is better than agreement with evil. We have to make sure that our bid for togetherness is a true God-given unity based upon His word and His Spirit rather than some man-made cobbled alliance doomed to collapse and disintegrate.

Man-made strategy

"By what route shall we attack?" he asked.

"Through the Desert of Edom," he answered.

So the king of Israel set out with the king of Judah and the king of Edom. After a roundabout march of seven days, the army had no more water for themselves or for the animals with them.

"What!" exclaimed the king of Israel. "Has the Lord called us three kings together only to hand us over to Moab?"

But Jehoshaphat asked, "Is there no prophet of the Lord here, that we may inquire of the Lord through him?"

An officer of the king of Israel answered, "Elisha son of Shaphat is here. He used to pour water on the hands of Elijah" (2 Kings 3:8-11).

Here is the church making prayerless plans which they expect God to bless. "By what route shall we attack?" asked the king of Moab. Not an unreasonable question. You'd think two pious kings from Israel would have considered that God might have something to say on the issue. But no. Instead, the brilliant proposal is put forward that they embark upon a long arduous march around the southern end of the Dead Sea, then up through Edomite territory in order to take Moab by surprise. They were in for a few surprises themselves. Their canteens were soon finished, and the tongues of both men and horses were swollen with thirst and sticking to the roofs of their mouths. Death seemed imminent. The expedition didn't look like such a brilliant idea any more. Neither do some of the enterprises launched by the church. We may look like people on the move with a mission, but so often we end up dried, shriveled, and desiccated, even on the very verge of death. And why? Could it be that we run our passionate crusades (for moral reform, multiplied conversions, and church growth) independently of God? "What!" exclaimed the king of Israel. "Has the LORD called us three kings together only to hand us over to Moab?" At last God gets a mention. The fear of God begins to enter the picture. God help us if we have to be brought to such drought and desolation before we begin to look up to the true source of guidance and power. Let's take our cue from Jehoshaphat. "Is there no prophet of the LORD here, that we may inquire of the Lord through him?" The church must arise to her true calling and destiny in God. She is to be a prophetic community upon a prophetic mission; a people who know how to hear God's voice and how to act upon it.

The prophet Elisha—spiritual clarity

The scene now begins to change. At last their dependency begins to shift in the right direction. A king in their company has asked for a prophet, and a soldier in the ranks knows of one worth listening to: "Elisha son of Shaphat is here. He used to pour water on the hands of Elijah." And so Elisha once again steps into the picture. Wouldn't you like to have something of his reputation? Five things should characterize the lives of those whom God would use, as He used Elisha, at a time when men became desperate for answers and began to turn to God.

1. You should be someone men think of when they want to find out what God says

It is possible to visit church after church and never truly hear a word from God. Let's make sure that this is not true in your town. Let's make sure that there is at least one preacher an inquirer could come to and hear God's unmistakable word.

2. You should be someone whom God has prepared by apprenticeship and who is now ready to play your part

We examined this issue in Chapter 3. It is significant that the officer pointed out that Elisha "used to pour water on the hands of Elijah." Joram's officer knew of Elisha's reputation. He knew who had trained Elisha. He knew that a man discipled by Elijah could be relied upon to speak the truth, and nothing but the truth. Jehoshaphat agreed, "The word of the LORD is with him" (v 12). It takes years of faithful service and unobtrusive loyalty to God and to your leaders in the LORD, to acquire a reputation like that. One day your hour of destiny will come, so in the meantime be faithful, get ready, prepare yourself and hang around a few Elijahs.

3. You should be someone who is fiercely independent of toadying flattery or compromise

> Elisha said to the king of Israel, "What do we have to do with each other? Go to the prophets of your father and the prophets of your mother.'
>
> "No," the king of Israel answered, "because it was the LORD who called us three kings together to hand us over to Moab."
>
> Elisha said, "As surely as the LORD Almighty lives, whom I serve, if I did not have respect for the presence of Jehoshaphat king of Judah, I would not look at you or even notice you. But now bring me a harpist" (2 Kings 3:13-15).

There is no cringing before royalty or fawning before the rich and famous here! Elisha is fearless. He has been in the presence of God, so he is not impressed by the persona of men. We need more of Elisha's outspoken directness and clarity. The world may not like what courageous men and women have to say, but they will at least be compelled to listen. We need the same unshackled vitality as Elisha if we are to command a hearing.

Elisha comes across as a man who is in charge: he comes from a higher court than that of King Joram. He taunts Joram, rubbing his nose in the emptiness of his phony religion and his phony prophets, "Shouldn't you send for some of your state priests and inherited ancestral prophets? Won't Daddy's court jesters do? Couldn't you hire some of Mommy's clairvoyants?" There are times when it's right to highlight the bankruptcy of the world's religions and their fabulous gurus. Men and women are not truly ready to listen to the authentic voice of God until they have shut their ears to the false voices of the "gods." They may not like us, but let's make sure they respect us. Let's be people of integrity; people who are faithful both to God and to the souls of men.

It is time haughty and frivolous rulers learned that the church is not some mental and moral police force, some wing of state power, which kings can simply use to help keep the people in order. The church is not birthed, governed, fed, maintained, and then buried by some act of Parliament. The church is first and foremost the servant of God, not of the State. The church in these last days must fight for her right to speak out for God.

4. You should be someone who cultivates sensitivity to the Spirit of God

> "But now bring me a harpist." While the harpist
> was playing, the hand of the LORD came upon
> Elisha and he said, "This is what the LORD says
> ..." (v 15).

You may feel yourself ready to speak, but what are you going to say? Elisha didn't think Joram deserved any word from God, let alone directives on how to redeem his present situation. It was for Jehoshaphat's sake alone that Elisha stirred up the gift that was in him. "As surely as the LORD Almighty lives, whom I serve, if I did not have respect for the presence of Jehoshaphat king of Judah, I would not look at you or even notice you" (v 14). Left to himself he would have delivered a message far different from the one that actually came, but Elisha was a man sensitive to the Holy Spirit.

Notice the place of music in this. A minstrel was summoned to strike up a tune, possibly the melody of one of David's psalms. Instrumental and vocal worship has a very vital role in inviting the presence of the Holy Spirit upon the lives of individuals and gatherings of God's people. This is part of the reason why Satan attacks the worship activities of the church. Worship brings down the anointing of God's Spirit; it is an invitation for God to move, and very often the occasion for Him to move.

See here, too, the place of special anointing. "The hand of the LORD came upon Elisha" (v 15). This was a fresh afflatus or impetus of the Spirit for this particular occasion. We should all look out for that. There are two perspectives on the gifts of the Spirit: one is the possessional view (that the believer has them all the time); the other is the occasional view (that they come as special manifestations as the need arises). Both views are true and can be argued from Scripture. Prophecies, healings, and miracles in particular are more occasional than possessional. We should expect them and look for them. The flow of the supernatural among us is something we should look for on a regular basis. The Methodist leader Samuel Chadwick said, "The church that does not work miracles is dead and ought to be buried."

5. You should be someone who will speak out clearly what God says to His people

> . . . and he said, "This is what the LORD says: Make this valley full of ditches. For this is what the Lord says: You will see neither wind nor rain, yet this valley will be filled with water, and you, your cattle and your other animals will drink. This is an easy thing in the eyes of the LORD; he will also hand Moab over to you. You will overthrow every fortified city and every major town. You will cut down every good tree, stop up all the springs,

and ruin every good field with stones."

The next morning, about the time for offering the sacrifice, there it was—water flowing from the direction of Edom! And the land was filled with water (2 Kings 3:16-20).

"Dig ditches. Attack and overthrow Moab." That was the essence of Elisha's word from God. A beautiful dovetailing of God's sovereignty and human responsibility. The Lord's provision for our desperate needs is a gift, but we have to dig ditches in order to receive and to contain what He gives. If, for example, the coming blessings of revival, which so many expect to come upon our nation, are to be stored—if our churches are truly to welcome and hold a great influx of converts from the neighborhoods around us, then we must get ready. Present structures and present avenues of service, nurture, and after-care may not be adequate when that time comes. It is hard work digging ditches. We must not begrudge the time, labor, expense, and effort involved. Our churches need proper foundations in belief and experience to be re-laid in some cases. We must raise up far more gifted and trained leaders than we can presently see. We surely need to work on our giving, our hospitality, our levels of friendship, our teaching, and our counseling skills if God is going to slake our thirst for fresh growth in raw converts. This may mean change: we may have to rid ourselves of archaic traditions and cumbersome procedures. Our style of worship, type and frequency of meetings, content and delivery of preaching may all need renewal. Can we really expect late-twentieth-century converts to walk in to fifteenth-century buildings, to recite sixteenth-century prayers, listen to a seventeenth-century Bible read by a minister in an eighteenth-century gown, and sing nineteenth-century hymns? Shouldn't some of our church life show that Christianity is as vibrant and up to date now as it was in all those previous centuries?

If this expectation of revival meets with skepticism in some, do note the fact that the water this army longed for came suddenly and in copious amounts at the time of the early morning sacrifice, "there it was—water flowing from the direction of Edom! And the land was filled with water" (v 20). This is typical of the way God works.

As for the direction to attack, do remember that all Joram wanted was a return to the status quo, a renewal of his annual tribute in mutton and wool. What God told him to do, however, was to pursue a course which military tacticians call a "scorched earth policy." This involved the blitzing of every town, the felling of every tree, the spiking of every well, and the ruination of every field. This would take Moab back to the Stone Age, at least for some considerable time. Sometimes God Himself is not very environmentally friendly. God is not soft on sin.

One thing was clear. This was not about to lead to a quick resumption of Moabite tribute payments to Joram's royal coffers. But then the job of a renewed church is not so much comfort as readiness: readiness to receive whatever spiritual blessing God chooses to give us, and to make total warfare upon the enemies of God.

The Moabite counterattack—spiritual conflict

Many people are offended by the warfare ordered by God when the Hebrews entered the Promised Land: "You must destroy them totally. Make no treaty with them and show them no mercy. . . . This is what you are to do to them. Break down their altars, smash their sacred stones, cut down their Asherah poles and burn their idols in the fire" (Deut. 7:1-6). In those days the only way to separate evil demons from their evil hosts the Hittites, Gurgashites, Ammonites, Canaanites, Perizzites, Hirites, and Jebusites was to make brutal warfare upon them.

Since the cross and resurrection of Jesus our weapons appear much more gentle, but are in fact devastatingly more effective. Now we praise, preach, persuade, and pray those demons out. It is not likely God will order His church to duplicate what Joram was told to do to Moab, and yet there are some lessons to learn here. The real enemy the church now faces is not so much hostile people, as the hostile demons within those people.

Just like the Moabites who faced the three kings that day, our spiritual enemies are numerous, determined, and prepared to fight. Where are these demons? They are just outside your skin! So close that you can regularly hear their lying whispers in your mind. Like the Moabites they are on the lookout for any chink of weakness or vulnerability within you. They love to see our in-fighting; nothing gives them greater pleasure than the thought that we have shed each other's blood by criticism, slander, misrepresentation, and outright schism (v 23). All the Moabites saw was an optical illusion, the reflection of the rising sun on the water-filled ditches. Let's make sure that our seeming weakness is an optical illusion too. The Moabites did not reckon on fresh water in the Israelite camp, and doubtless the devil isn't reckoning on fresh supplies of the Spirit in the church either. It would be wonderful to disappoint him, wouldn't it?

See, too, how the Moabite attack focused upon one of the alliance leaders, the king of Edom (v 26). Pray for your leaders, for they are a prey to sickness, marital tension, unclean sexual thoughts, depression, and deception. The Moabites even resorted to human sacrifice in order to coax unseen powers to help them win the day (v 27). Human sacrifice has been a feature of all demonized cultures throughout human history. The Canaanites, Egyptians, Carthaginians, Romans, Druids, Goths, Vikings, Aztecs, Hindus, and Chinese have all practiced it. In our own century the communists in Russia, China, Vietnam, and South America have all practiced it. Western civilization aborts unborn babies at the rate of one every three seconds, and it is said that some Satanists aim to sacrifice human children in order to bring about the total defeat of Christ's church. The whole of Satan's empire is founded upon death, usually the deaths of the innocent. His victims are without number.

That is why Christians must be willing to die. We cannot win any war in which we are overanxious to save our own skin. God sent His own Son to become the victim of Satan's murderous hatred of God and his government. It was by that death that Satan was defeated. We are called to reinforce that victory of the cross. We do so registering our willingness to die if necessary. "They overcame him [the dragon] by the blood of the Lamb and by the word of their testimony; they did not love their lives so much as to shrink from death" (Rev. 12:11). You and I must be prepared ruthlessly to destroy the devil and all his works and to carry out completely, at whatever cost, the directions God gives us. Otherwise we will encounter an even greater determination to beat us back. There is power in sacrifice: the Moabite king sacrificed his firstborn son and thus released a demonic backlash of fury against the Israelites that was so intense it caused the retreat of the Israelite forces.

Only a church which has broken with compromise, embraced the clarity that comes with the prophetic word, and is prepared for all-out conflict will be able to stand in the intense spiritual warfare about to come upon the earth. This is the message of Elisha and the tale of three kings.

6 COMPANY WIDOW DISCOVERS OIL

2 Kings 4:1-7

Down and out

The next episode in Elisha's ministry is a "rags to riches" story which opens in a scene of misery, impoverishment, and despair. One of the company of the prophets had died, and his widow had been left penniless. The poor woman was in a terrible state. Her money was gone, the family was in debt, and her two sons were in jeopardy of being sold into slavery to pay off her remaining creditor. This woman was not only down, she was very nearly out.

The state of the church

> The wife of a man from the company of the prophets cried out to Elisha, "Your servant my husband is dead, and you know that he revered the Lord. But now his creditor is coming to take my two boys as his slaves" (2 Kings 4:1).

This is the sad condition of so many of God's people. They live with a mood of loss because their best days seem to be behind them. Like the widow, these people are miserable. Yet we all know that Christianity is a religion of joy, not of misery. We all know that a mood of despair and dejection such as this poor woman felt is not the mood of authentic biblical Christianity. The great Methodist leader, John Wesley, said that

> sour godliness is the devil's religion. It does not owe its inception to truly spiritual people or to truly spiritual practice. I suspect that sour godliness originated among unhappy, semi-religious people who had just enough religion to make them miserable but not enough to do them good!

He was right. Whenever you see a soured, miserable, and despairing attitude among God's people you know that an enemy has been at work. Death has crept in to your experience many times no doubt, and you have often felt "widowed" or cut off from your source of security, happiness, and joy. Whole churches and denominations can end up like this widow.

Sometimes it is because the church has been wedded for years to a false and unbiblical outlook in both belief and practice. Someone has said, "Marry the spirit of the age in this generation and you will be a widow in the next." So many have been wedded to dated philosophies and psychology which have shaped their beliefs; for example, skepticism about the supernatural element in the Bible, or Freudian techniques in the counseling of those in trouble. As philosophical outlooks move on, the church is left widowed.

At other times fine leaders, preachers, pastors, and theologians are removed by death and the church is left feeling bereft. Where are their successors? Where are the Luthers, Calvins, Wesleys, Whitefields, Finneys, Spurgeons, and Lloyd-Joneses of today? In asking this, the church feels widowed and deserted.

Some feel that even Christ has abandoned us to our lukewarm compromise.

There is some truth in each one of these descriptions. We do sense Christ's absence, and we do feel abandoned at times to bankrupt philosophies and leaderless meandering. We sense that our spiritual capital is running out. The church in spiritual widowhood is on the way to spiritual destitution, and we are all too aware of our poverty. We sense we have little to give to a needy world around us. We cannot properly feed ourselves, let alone the spiritually hungry crowds in our parishes. Obligated to give so much, we seem at times to possess so little. We are in the grip of debts we cannot pay. The Bible says that debt is a form of slavery, "The rich rule over the poor, and the borrower is servant to the lender" (Prov. 22:7).

If, cap in hand, Christian people go begging to the world for their faith, their finances, their following, and their freedom then it will not be long before those same creditors make us acutely aware that far from being free, we are, in fact, in slavery. When Christian people are full of fear, afraid to speak out their true beliefs lest they cause offense, and unable to take independent action in case their funding is cut, then those people are truly in slavery no matter how much they sing about their freedom.

The first people to suffer are the children. So often the children of the faithful are carried off as slaves—slaves to peer pressure, slaves to the fashions, diversions, entertainment, and pathetic goals of their pagan contemporaries. These same kids are bored with church and its powerless religion. They know instinctively that somewhere along the line we sold out to some evil creditor instead of selling out to the LORD. In spite of their own rebellion against this, and their vaunted anger with "the system," these kids are themselves sold out to the same spirit of the age. They ape the world's morals, speak in its language, pursue its ambitions, and indulge in its illicit pleasures. The creditor wanted both of the widow's children. You can be equally sure that he's eager to have all of yours.

This then is the state of much of the church. She is in bondage along with her children (Gal. 4:25) because she has sold out to the wrong kind of creditor. Can anything be done about this?

It's time to get desperate

The answer to that question very much depends upon how desperate we are. In waking up to her plundered and pitiable condition, this widow awoke to reality. The church in many quarters needs to do the same. In turning to God's prophet Elisha, she was also turning to God in her trouble. The church needs to do the same. Elisha was God's representative, and in making her plea to Elisha, she was stating her needs to God. God is looking for this kind of praying from His people. It is prayer which is marked by genuine grief and earnest determination. This lady meant business, and so should we. Watch her present her case to Elisha.

1. She reminded herself of her former advantages when her husband was alive

She said, "Your servant my husband is dead, and you know that he revered the Lord." She knew that she could not live on those past glories; that she could not live the life of faith by proxy. Her husband's life before God had served to keep predatory wolves from her door, but her husband was dead and those wolves had begun to burst into the former security of her dwelling through every crack of vulnerability and weakness. Fear, ruin, poverty, further bereavement, and captivity all threatened her. We can have just enough religion to make us decent but not enough to make us dynamic. This woman resolved to move out in a first-hand faith of her own.

2. She faced honestly the misery of her present condition

"The creditor is coming to take my two boys as his slaves." She faced the facts. She did not indulge in the make-believe and semi-confident cover-ups of so many believers today. It's possible to move the chairs around, update the music, raise our hands in worship, and serve doughnuts and coffee after the service and tell ourselves that because the meetings are brighter, then they must also be getting better. This may not be so. Many who profess to be interested in *charismatic* renewal are pursuing only *cosmetic* or surface change. They are not interested in a recovery of New Testament structure, ministry, and life within their churches. The American preacher Vance Havner said, "The church is so subnormal that if it ever got back to the New Testament normal it would seem to people to be abnormal." Let's face the facts of our desperate need for change.

3. She cried out to God to intervene

There is such a thing as a divine discontentment, and wherever it occurs people shake off respectability and become desperate. I have talked with church leaders who have calmly reported the fact that they have seen no conversions in their churches for over a year and they are not desperate about it. Amazing? No . . . tragic!

It is this kind of desperation alone which draws the attention of Almighty God. Back in 1540, Frederick Myconius, a friend and assistant to the reformer Martin Luther, fell seriously ill. He declined rapidly to the point of imminent death and dictated a farewell letter to his master, Luther. But this was not the last word on the issue. Luther wrote back immediately in these words, "I command thee in the Name of God to live, because I still have need of thee in the work of reforming the Church. . . . The LORD will never let me hear that thou art dead, but will permit thee to survive me. For this I am praying. This is my will, and my will be done, because I seek only to glorify God." Myconius had lost the power of speech by the time the letter came, but its arrival had a remarkable effect upon him. His spirit revived, his body recovered, and he went on to live for six more years, surviving Luther himself by two months. Luther's desperation caught the attention of God.

Faith of this kind always does. God must have given Luther His full attention.

God can do it again

Elisha certainly gave this widow his full attention. "How can I help you?" he asked, and then inquired, "Tell me what do you have in your house?" We can perceive that God is about to reverse the situation. Elisha has been given divine directions to pursue this line with her. Of course, at this stage the situation does not look very promising, for she has nothing but a small flask containing a little oil. But this is the key. Oil is a symbol of the Holy Spirit, and the fact that this woman has only a little becomes the pledge that she shall have more.

God has never deserted His church. We are men and women of the Spirit, and the fact that we see and experience any of the Spirit's operations and activities among us is also an opening for the possibility that we can see more. First, however, we have to begin to think big.

> Elisha said, "Go round and ask all your neighbors for empty jars. Don't ask for just a few. Then go inside and shut the door behind you and your sons. Pour oil into all the jars, and as each is filled, put it to one side" (vv 3-4).

"Don't ask for just a few." Expect an abundance. In the United Kingdom we think that a church of 200 people is a big church, that the cure of a common cold is a major miracle, and that the provision of enough funds to pay our quarterly bills is a financial breakthrough. We think small, we believe small, and our expectations are trivial. God wanted to give this woman as much oil as she asked for, or at least, as much oil as she made provision for in her preparation and build-up to the divine intervention.

Oil is a symbol of the presence and activity of the Holy Spirit. It was used as fuel for light in every Hebrew household in order to banish the darkness. It was frequently rubbed upon wounds, sores, and other external injuries as a healing agent (Mark. 6:13; James 5:14), as well as being administered as a mild laxative from time to time in the case of internal gastric and intestinal disorders. In Leviticus 14:10-18, oil was a major ingredient in the special offerings prescribed to announce the complete cleansing of a leper, and as such it symbolized the removal of the physical, psychological, and socially damaging effects of this disease. Oil was used in the cooking of food, thus supplying taste, aroma, and nourishment to the meal. It was applied as an anointing on the heads of kings at their inauguration, as a symbol of the power and authority of the Spirit of God coming upon them to equip them for their task (1 Sam. 10:1; 1 Kings 1:39). A similar anointing was applied to both priests and prophets in their service, showing their need for divine power. Lastly, oil was a factor in ministering both internal and external beauty upon God's people—it symbolized gladness of heart (Isa. 61:3) and cosmetic attractiveness for head and skin, so that outer appearance could tally with inner happiness (Ruth 3:3; 2 Sam. 12:20).

This is a rich and suggestive spectrum of meaning. It tells us that God wants to give His people, His church today, an abundance of power to enable them to throw back the forces of darkness. We must become a people marked by joy and celebration; a people who are becoming progressively whole within ourselves and who can point out for others the way to God's physical, psychological, and spiritual healing in their lives. God wants to anoint us with authority to pray, pronounce, and preach for Him so that heaven's power is released to effect changes in the world.

How to strike oil

It is instructive to observe some of the details of how this abundance came into the widow's life. The narrative says,

She left him and afterward shut the door behind her
and her sons. They brought the jars to her and she
kept pouring. When all the jars were full, she said to
her son, "Bring me another one." But he replied,
"There is not a jar left." Then the oil stopped flowing. She went and told the man of God, and he said,
"Go, sell the oil and pay your debts. You and your
sons can live on what is left" (2 Kings 4:5-7).

1. She did what she was told

Even though the orders were unusual, she didn't worry about
what the neighbors would think. Someone has said, "One of the
reasons people find it hard to obey the commands of Christ is
because they don't like taking orders from a stranger." Well, Jesus is
no stranger to us, and though His orders sometimes seem strange,
let's learn to do what He says.

2. She prepared for abundance

Elisha told her, "Don't ask for just a few." It would appear she
cleared the village out of every pot, pan, jar, and bottle she could
find. Have you got rid of your "just a few" mentality? Our
expectancy may be the only limitation on what God is prepared to
do for us.

3. By faith, she used what she had

It seemed silly, pouring out her few fluid ounces of oil from one
flask into another. She started where she was, not where she would
have liked to be. She used what she had, not what she had not. She
stepped out with little and God turned it into much. Jesus said, "If
you have faith as small as a mustard seed, you can say to this
mulberry tree, 'Be uprooted and planted in the sea,' and it will obey
you" (Luke 17:6). It would appear then that it doesn't matter how
much faith we have, so long as we use what we have got.

4. She did this in private before she went public

All this went on behind closed doors. Sometimes God has His people prove His greatness in privacy before we announce to the world and "sell" off what we have received. We restore our own family life before we presume to counsel others. We build our own sense of community before we invite others to join it. We see God's power at work healing sick or demonized saints before we minister it to unbelievers.

God answered her prayer. Mark Twain once said, "I don't know a single product that enters our country untaxed except for answered prayer." There are no trade restrictions on God's answers to believing prayer. The Lord has seen our plight. The moment we see it too, and come to Him for His supply, then He will set in motion the miracle of His provision. For the widow, the complex molecules of a small volume of oil were multiplied. For us, an even greater miracle is required—we need the oil of the Holy Spirit in renewal, reformation, restoration, and revival. It is God's express desire to give us enough to meet our own needs and to have plenty left over to give for the need of others. The only limitation appears to be the number of clean, empty vessels which we can present.

When we have plenty of oil, we won't need to advertise the fact, people will come running. There is no discovery in life like the discovery of oil. It leads to debt cancellation on a grand scale and debt cancellation is what the gospel is all about. The gospel is good news for the poor.

This then was the widow's rags to riches story. It can be yours too.

HOW TO RAISE A DEAD KID

2 Kings 4:8-37

How to raise a dead kid? We don't need much instruction on that, do we? We're pretty good at that already. We raise kids who are dead enough as it is—dead to the joys of life, dead to the purpose of life, dead to the God of life, dead to everything meaningful and vital. You can see it in their eyes. Death. They are surly, rebellious, critical, jaded, worldly-wise, and world-weary. They've been there, seen it, and bought the T-shirt. Nothing really excites them anymore. They can't see the point. They seem to have given up on life. They seem to have died prematurely.

Better rephrase that, then: "How to raise a dead kid—to life." That's what we really mean; that's what we really need to hear. This is what the next episode in Elisha's life is all about. It concerns the prophet's role in supernaturally reversing a situation of infertility in the life of a wealthy but childless couple. Indirectly, Elisha helped them to conceive. Later, tragedy intervened and the miracle child, the surprise gift from God, died. Elisha again became involved and in doing so acted as a powerful demonstration of how to raise a dead kid to life.

The raising of the next generation properly is crucial to the fulfillment of God's purposes today. Parents need all the wisdom they can get to help them carry out that task well.

Loving the things we love

A father was Christmas shopping. He stood in a large toy shop and after some thought chose a beautiful working model train. The workmanship was exquisite, and the railway engine not only looked good, it whistled, belched smoke, and made realistic noises as it moved. "I'll take it," he said to the assistant. She smiled and replied, "Thank you, sir. I'm sure that your son will love it." The father thought for a moment and then said, "Mmmm . . . yes . . . you're quite right. Maybe you'd better give me two of them. I wouldn't want him to be envious or disappointed!"

Sometimes it is easy to get our children to love the things we love, but there are times when it presents a much more serious challenge. Are your children growing in their love for the Lord, his people, the Bible, your Christian values, and your biblical world-view? It is gratifying when they share our hobbies, enjoy our tastes in films, books, and music, or take equal pleasure in our friends, house, or garden. But any Christian parent has ambitions which flow much deeper and much more powerfully than these. We want our children to love our God and to experience His life.

Three basic convictions

It is very important then that Christian parents, especially the parents of young children, grasp three basic convictions. First, they need to be convinced that the new birth is always original and never inherited. God has no grandchildren. Because you are born again, it does not follow that your children will automatically be so. New life flows directly from the Holy Spirit and not indirectly through the parents" blood (John 1:12-13). Our children have real privileges if they have been born into a Christian home, but God starts over afresh each time one of them comes to experience the birth from above.

Second, believing parents need to know that a home of authentic spirituality is the best environment for our children if we truly wish to see them come to life. Children can quickly sniff out religious hypocrisy and unreality, more quickly than a cat can sniff out a dead fish. Unlike the cat, however, children are rapidly turned off by the whiff of dead religion. It really offends them and sets them up for the rejection of our decayed and decaying spirituality as soon as they are in a position to make up their minds for themselves.

Third, we need to be encouraged that we are not alone in this task. God has raised up other agencies to come alongside us and help. Parents are in partnership with others who have a special ministry under God to convey life to our children. Both parents and "children's workers" are given prominence in this story. We are going to look at the respective roles of the home and the church in raising dead children to life. The story concerns one such child, the nameless boy given to the Shunammite and her husband.

The home and its ministry

The story begins before the boy was even born. It features a well-heeled middle-class couple who seem to have everything: large house, secure income, happy marriage, and all of their material needs met. Everything, that is, except a child to share this abundance with them. It is noteworthy that the husband is a background figure in the story. He may have taken a back seat in other respects also. It is possible, for example, that this man had little or no relationship with God. Many marriages are like this—a keen believing wife coupled with a nominally spiritual husband who is busy with his work, interests, and long-term career. This is not an ideal situation for a child, yet even when only one parent is converted, even if that parent is not the "head of the household," it still gives the child a tremendous advantage: "For the unbelieving husband has been sanctified through his wife. . . . Otherwise your children would be unclean, but as it is, they are holy" (1 Cor. 7:14).

Whether we have misjudged the Shunammite's husband or not we can make several comments about the characteristics of this particular home.

1. There was a love for God's Word in this home

> One day Elisha went to Shunem. And a well-to-do woman was there, who urged him to stay for a meal. So whenever he came by, he stopped there to eat (2 Kings 4:8).

If this display of hospitality to Elisha was typical, then it indicated a ready reception both for God's messenger and for God's message. At least one of the members of this marriage partnership was not only in sympathy with, but enthusiastic toward God's Word. The Word is the great life-giving and life-transforming agent, not only in our own lives but also in the lives of our children. According to Paul's statements about Timothy;

> I have been reminded of your sincere faith, which first lived in your grandmother Lois and in your mother Eunice and, I am persuaded, now lives in you also ... and how from infancy you have known the holy Scriptures, which are able to make you wise for salvation through faith in Christ Jesus (2 Tim. 1:5; 3:15).

Many children first learn the Word of God through their mother's agency—stories, answers to questions, countless hours of conversation and special readings. One pastor was once asked which version of the Bible he liked best, was it AV, RSV, or NIV? He replied, "I like the MMV—My Mother's Version, because she translated it into her life and I first came to see it was true by watching her."

2. There was a practical down-to-earth spirituality in this home

> She said to her husband, "I know that this man who often comes our way is a holy man of God. Let's make a small room on the roof and put in it a bed and a table, a chair and a lamp for him. Then he can stay there whenever he comes to us" (2 Kings 4:9-10).

This lady was very generous and very hospitable. She urged her husband to build a loft extension especially for the itinerant prophet, setting this room aside to make life more comfortable for the man of God. This is true hospitality as opposed to mere entertaining. In entertaining the focus is upon the hosts and their home, the furnishings, decor, and cordon-bleu cookery, which are all designed to impress the guests. In hospitality the focus is upon the comfort, pleasure, and refreshment of the visitor. Beans on toast before a blazing log fire may be all that is required, because the design here is to bless the guests. Many women with spark, initiative, and spiritual appetite, like this Shunammite, slide into a kind of super-spirituality which not only fawns on the men of God who come their way, but also acts with a patronizing contempt for their not-so-spiritual husbands. Not so with this woman. She was marked by submission, in that she fully consulted her husband's opinion and approval in this project. She respected his headship over her life both in word (the way she spoke *of* him and *to* him), and also in deed. She had no "little secrets" which she kept from him which would have led him into suspicion of her, her friendships, her activities, or her religion. And she was a good homemaker who made the guest room as pleasant, as welcoming, and as inviting as she possibly could. Major W. F. Batt used to say, "Holiness begins at home and sanctification at the sink. This is what we mean by a down-to-earth spirituality."

We know that God rewards genuine hospitality. Hebrews 13:2

says, "Do not forget to entertain strangers, for by so doing some people have entertained angels without knowing it." An angel is a messenger of God, and in the Old Testament many people took in strangers and found out later that the strangers were messengers of God. So whether the hosts were Abraham (Gen. 18:1ff), Gideon (Jud. 6:11ff) or Manoah (Jud. 13:2ff), each of these people found that their guest left more than he had taken—rich promises, powerful encouragement, and outstanding advice were just some of the blessings these angels left. The Shunammite found the same to be true in her case. The guest she blessed left a blessing with her too. Make this gift of hospitality a habit of your lifestyle. If God gives you children, one spin-off will be that your children are exposed over time to many wonderful men and women of God who will leave a deposit in your children's lives.

3. There was contentment and not bitterness in this home

> One day when Elisha came, he went up to his room and lay down there. He said to his servant Gehazi, "Call the Shunammite." So he called her, and she stood before him. Elisha said to him, "Tell her, 'You have gone to all this trouble for us. Now what can be done for you? Can we speak on your behalf to the king or the commander of the army?'" (2 Kings 4:11-13).

Elisha offered to use his influence with man to bring some material reward to this woman and her husband. Her reply is striking. She says in effect, "Thanks, but no thanks. We really do have all that we need" (v 13b). She knew when she was well-off, even though some people don't. She had a less than perfect husband, a detached house (with a loft extension!) on their own land, a nice bunch of friendly neighbors, a full larder, and cash to spare. She had no child, though, and this could mean the end of the family name and the loss of her inheritance had her husband died first. Yet she seemed content. No complaints. It is good to cultivate this joy in what we have rather than bitterness over what we don't have.

There can be no doubt that the longing for a child ran under the surface of her contentment, but she never allowed it to emerge in envy, resentment, and jealousy towards others. The Bible says, "Sons are a heritage from the Lord . . . blessed is the man whose quiver is full of them" (Ps. 127:3, 5). I can vouch for that. A quiverful was about six, and even with my half-quiverful I've been blessed incalculably. There can be no doubt she wanted a son, but it seems she'd given up hoping, for when Elisha promised her that she would hold one in her arms by the same time next year, she couldn't bear to be taunted, and couldn't rise to believe this astonishing promise. It was too good to be true.

The suppressed longing was fulfilled. The Lord often blesses us in surprising ways and at surprising times. I've seen God reverse infertility just as dramatically as this in answer to believing prayer and prophetic words. God knows our hearts and really does care about our secret frustrations. Even if you aren't as well-off as this couple, be content. God knows what you need.

4. There was a rich mothering instinct at work in this home

> The child grew, and one day he went out to his father, who was with the reapers. "My head! My head!" he said to his father. His father told a servant, "Carry him to his mother." After the servant had lifted him up and carried him to his mother, the boy sat on her lap until noon, and then he died. She went up and laid him on the bed of the man of God, then shut the door and went out (2 Kings 4:18-21).

The promised child was born, grew, and later fell suddenly and seriously ill. Was it a cerebral hemorrhage, a stroke, cerebral cancer, or the failure of some other vital organ? We don't know. But see how she nursed the child. She loved this boy and she let him know he was loved by the way she spoke to him, kissed him, and cared for him.

If you want your children to come to know what God is like as their heavenly Father then let them see it first in your parental love for them. So many youths and adults in our generation have grown up believing that "Father" is a dirty word and that God, if He exists at all, is some cold, distant, bad-tempered, inconsistent and tyrannical law-giver devoid of tenderness, feeling, and compassion. It is vital we invest time, love, care, and attention upon our children. The prophet Malachi said that God's end time prophetic Elijah would "turn the hearts of the fathers to their children" (Mal. 4:6). Parents, turn your heart toward home. We live in a time when children are seen as a curse and a liability to be dumped in day care or handed over to baby-sitters. Many parents give their children everything except themselves. The Bible teacher Stephen Olford said, "When hugging and kissing end in any home, trouble is on the way."

5. *There was a bold and active faith for the child in this home*

> She went up and laid him on the bed of the man of God, then shut the door and went out. She called her husband and said, "Please send me one of the servants and a donkey so I can go to the man of God quickly and return.'
>
> "Why go to him today?" he asked. "It's not the New Moon or the Sabbath."
>
> "It's all right," she said.
>
> She saddled the donkey and said to her servant, "Lead on; don't slow down for me unless I tell you." So she set out and came to the man of God at Mount Carmel. When he saw her in the

distance, the man of God said to his servant Gehazi, "Look! There's the Shunammite! Run to meet her and ask her," 'Are you all right? Is your husband all right? Is your child all right?' "

"Everything is all right," she said.

When she reached the man of God at the mountain, she took hold of his feet. Gehazi came over to push her away, but the man of God said, "Leave her alone! She is in bitter distress, but the LORD has hidden it from me and has not told me why."

"Did I ask you for a son, my lord?" she said. "Didn't I tell you," "Don't raise my hopes?" (2 Kings 4:21-28).

Again it was her faith and not her husband's which made the difference. The father had given up hope and could see no point in troubling the prophet Elisha. The Scriptures define faith as "being sure of what we hope for and certain of what we do not see" (Heb. 11:1). We can be grateful that this woman had that kind of faith. A persuasion of the possibility of unseen realities had entered into her heart by the Spirit. She could brook no delay and was prepared to travel some fifteen miles on the back of a donkey in order to request the ministry she knew that her deceased son most needed. When it comes to the special needs of our children we too may need to travel miles for the right church or school, involving ourselves in considerable effort or expense in order to secure our children's best interests. This is what biblical faith does. It affects lives. This woman's faith was going to affect her child's future in an astounding way. I once read, "By the time children are five, their parents will have done at least half of all that can ever be done to determine the children's future." There can be no doubt that this distraught mother had done her part.

And of course faith speaks. As she put her case to the prophet we can see faith's logic and eloquence (v 28). It made no sense to her for God to give her this precious child, only to snatch him back a few short years later. Six or seven years of life could not have been all God had in mind. She could picture the boy alive and well again. She knew where to go and whom to ask in order to make this miracle a reality. She knew God had plans for this precious life He had so remarkably given and she clung to the belief that Elisha could raise him from the dead, in order for those plans to be realized in her son's life ("the child's mother said, 'As surely as the LORD lives and as you live, I will not leave you'" v 30).

John and Charles Wesley had a mother who prayed individually each day for all of her seventeen children. She spoke intimately and directly to each one concerning their spiritual condition, and she urged upon them all the necessity of genuine repentance, personal conversion and faith. Wesley said of her, "I learned more of Christianity from my mother than from all the theologians of England." Those of us who are parents can imitate the example of these "mothers in Israel." Don't live in expectancy of your children's rebellion against your faith. Instead, believe God for His calling upon their lives. Don't prepare for disaster, prepare for their destiny. This lady was not planning for a funeral but for a resurrection. She laid the corpse out not in the "chapel of rest" at the local undertakers, but in the prophet's room where someone could really "undertake" for her grief and her need! This is what it means to dedicate our children to the Lord by faith.

Whatever prayers you pray for your children, make sure they include prayers full of faith expectancy for their spiritual resurrection. "There is no more influential or powerful role on earth than a mother's . . . their words are never fully forgotten, their touch leaves an indelible impression, and the memory of their presence lasts a lifetime."[1]

But what of the other agencies God uses to influence our children towards His power and His life?

The church and its ministry

One of the greatest things we as parents can do for our children is to bring them into an atmosphere charged with faith because it is filled with the presence of men and women of faith. Each one of our children is a unique, unrepeatable, and precious gift of God. Nobody knew that better than the Shunammite. But she also knew that until God touches them, they are dead to real life, life as God intended it to be; just as this poor child was, laid out in Elisha's motel room. They are spiritually dead, and they are on their way to eternal death unless something intervenes to prevent this.

The problem is not just "in the head" though it may appear so at first: 'My head! My head!' he said to his father" (v 19), as if it were merely an intellectual difficulty which could be solved by the application of the appropriate educational methodology. Our children need more than a good education; they need total regeneration. It is important to point out, however, that regeneration is not a matter of superstition. There is possibly a hint of superstition in this mother's actions. She laid the body on the bed of the man of God. Was she thinking in terms of special places, special times, and even of some special ceremony to be performed? Whether she was or not, we cannot place our trust in splashes of holy water, signing with a cross, holding them in our arms, laying hands on their head, attending the right classes or meeting in church on the correct day of the week. Our children need a touch from God or all else will be to no avail.

What this mother instinctively knew, I'm sure, was that godly people must have input into the lives of our children, and therefore it is essential for them to be exposed to the anointed ministry of properly authorized servants of God.

What is this "anointed ministry" and who are these servants of God? To answer that question we need only look at the attitudes and actions of Elisha and, by way of contrast, those of his servant

101

Gehazi. There are many challenges for children's and youth workers in church life today. I'd like to list them in a series of imperatives
for all those involved in the church's ministry to children and
young people.

1. *Be genuinely concerned*

> So she set out and came to the man of God at
> Mount Carmel. When he saw her in the distance,
> the man of God said to his servant Gehazi, "Look!
> There's the Shunammite! Run to meet her and ask
> her, 'Are you all right? Is your husband all right? Is
> your child all right?'"
>
> "Everything is all right," she said (2 Kings
> 4:25-26).

Elisha is no mere functionary, a man with a job to do, a
mechanical "layer-on-of-hands" for sick babies. He is genuinely
interested in the child's welfare. As soon as he became aware of the
likelihood of a problem, he was anxious to know the facts and to
find out if he could help. There is an urgency in this. He is at haste
to find out the family's needs first hand, and so he sends his speed-
ier servant Gehazi to rush on ahead and make the necessary
inquiries. It is striking that Gehazi's questions are fobbed off with
merely polite replies. There was something cold, perfunctory, and
terribly formal about his manner. The woman would not open her
heart to him. Anonymity and impersonalism do not help in any
children's ministry: we need to know our children's teachers and
they need to know us. Those same leaders must be genuinely
concerned about the youngsters in their charge—they must try to
match the parents" concern for the child's spiritual welfare with
their own. Elisha shows the way.

2. Be real

> When she reached the man of God at the mountain, she took hold of his feet. Gehazi came over to push her away, but the man of God said, "Leave her alone! She is in bitter distress, but the LORD has hidden it from me and has not told me why" (2 Kings 4:27).

There is something very warm and approachable in the humanity of Elisha. This mother can take hold of his feet, and observing that action, Elisha instantly discerns the seriousness of the situation and wells up with sympathy. He is eager to listen. We have not misjudged Gehazi, though. Gehazi is left cold by these displays of emotion and with false ideas of propriety he hastily shoves the woman aside.

I have a minister friend who had the impertinence to move the Communion table six inches back to make room for the children to stand and sing from the platform on a Sunday School anniversary. Hauled before the deacons that week, he was publicly rebuked and charged to apply to them in writing if he ever wished to repeat the same action again. Presumably this offended their sense of religious propriety. Gehazi would have been proud of them.

Harshness of this kind is a big turn-off to children. Children are left cold (we might say "cold-dead") by a plastic piety of this sort with its silly scruples, and rules of procedure ("In writing, in triplicate please, and we'll see what we can do!"). For God's sake be real! Be a friend for those to whom you minister.

3. Be wholehearted

> Elisha said to Gehazi, "Tuck your cloak into your belt, take my staff in your hand and run. If you meet anyone, do not greet him, and if anyone

103

greets you, do not answer. Lay my staff on the boy's face."

But the child's mother said, "As surely as the LORD lives and as you live, I will not leave you." So he got up and followed her.

Gehazi went on ahead and laid the staff on the boy's face, but there was no sound or response. So Gehazi went back to meet Elisha and told him, "The boy has not awakened."

When Elisha reached the house, there was the boy lying dead on his couch. He went in, shut the door on the two of them and prayed to the LORD. Then he got on the bed and lay upon the boy, mouth to mouth, eyes to eyes, hands to hands. As he stretched himself out upon him, the boy's body grew warm (2 Kings 4:29-34).

It gets worse. Gehazi is a model of "how not to do it." Elisha sends him on ahead yet once more with the staff of his spiritual authority and strict orders to go straight to the boy and apply the means of God's power: "Lay my staff on the boy's face." Gehazi dutifully carries out his orders in the detached, precise, and mechanical way which we have by now come to expect of him. He is indifferent about results. He lays the divinely authorized instrument down on the body, stands passively by, and when nothing happens, duly returns with the disappointing "mission report" to Elisha, but feels no disappointment. "The boy has not awakened" ("Well, what did he expect?" we can hear him asking under his breath. "Resurrection or something?"). When the instrument of power doesn't work he gives up quickly.

We need to feel the compassion of God. In this connection it is striking how frequently the New Testament uses the verb *splanchnizomai* to refer to the compassion of God. The majority of the twelve instances describe Jesus" motivation in ministering healing, or other bursts of divine power, to those in need. The verb is very graphic indeed. The noun form of the verb was commonly used to refer to the inner organs of mankind, particularly those in the lower abdomen—the intestines in a man, the womb in a woman. This signifies that Jesus felt emotion deeply, "in His guts," whenever He saw men and women in desperate need. Unless you and I have felt similarly "gutted" in our ministry, then it is unlikely that we will ever be used by God to any great effect. We must feel the worth of those to whom we minister, especially if they are children.

The great evangelist D. L. Moody once reported that he had just returned from a meeting where he had seen two-and-half conversions! He was asked, did he mean two adults and one child? "No," he replied, "I mean two children and one adult. The adult's life was already half over, the children had their whole lives still before them to be lived for God." Moody had a true sense of the worth of a child. It is important that children's workers make sure that the fire of their love for children does not go out. Elisha, by way of contrast, stirs up the gifts within him. He gives the fire of his prophetic love and prophetic sensitivity a good stoke: "He went in, shut the door on the two of them and prayed to the LORD" (v 33). Elisha is looking intensely for God's strategy, the divine key to this child's need. He will not accept the first disappointing results.

Elisha was not afraid to do the unusual. What was so unusual? Elisha didn't only lay his staff, he laid himself on the child, having asked the Lord how best to minister. He didn't lean on the child (some teachers try bribery, manipulation, and coercion to achieve results), he lay on the child. He didn't just give the truth, he gave himself. He so identified with the cold, stiffened corpse of the boy, that warmth went from his body into the body of the boy, and breath went from his mouth into the airless airways and nostrils of the child.

This is real children's ministry. The child must not only feel the truth we preach, he must feel the warmth of our spirit coming with that truth. What you are is nearly as important as what you say. Elisha really meant business and so should we. So far as it depended upon Elisha, the child would live.

4. Be yourself

> Elisha turned away and walked back and forth in
> the room and then got on the bed and stretched
> out upon him once more. The boy sneezed seven
> times and opened his eyes (2 Kings 4:35).

Having beseeched God for a strategy, Elisha beseeched God for a result. We see him pacing back and forth and then repeating the whole exercise yet again (v 35)! Sometimes it is important simply to persevere in what God has told you to do.

We have already noted how Elisha gave of himself to this dead child. It is important to see that he also gave himself, his total personality. He stepped out of his dignity as the "man of God" and broke religious and social propriety to do so. To work with children you must make contact at whatever point you can. In Elisha's case it was "mouth to mouth, eyes to eyes, hands to hands." In our case it will be with our humor, with our time, with our sense of fun, with appropriate music, with ingenious visual aids, with our playfulness, sense of care, and openness. Let the children near to you. All this may not be very dignified, but it is essential.

God wants to use you

God does not simply lob His blessings over the Milky Way. God works through real people like you and me. Life is imparted to a child not through an impersonal instrument like a stick, but through a personal one like you. So it is important to say to parents and youth workers alike: don't merely give children the truth, give them yourself.

The result was very beautiful indeed. Elisha summoned the mother to see what was happening. "The child sneezed seven times." The breath came back in several short explosive bursts. It was all so naturally supernatural, and so supernaturally natural. The child wasn't coached to repeat the right answers; he just sneezed. It doesn't take years of experience or a high level of attainment in order to sneeze; it simply takes the presence of life. We don't need to look for a great deal of knowledge, an articulate testimony or great evidence of mighty exploits in a child, just the "sneeze" of unfeigned repentance and genuine faith in Jesus.

Child conversion doesn't take away children's enthusiasm for Superman, their silly sense of humor, their love for games and sweets, or their immature and often foolish behavior—it just opens their lives to a new dimension, to the love and power of Jesus. When that happens we as parents can honor the people God used—"She came in, fell at his feet and bowed to the ground"— and receive our kids to ourselves in a new way: "Then she took her son and went out."

How do you raise a dead kid . . . to life? Put him or her in the right home and take him to the right church and see what happens. Jesus is still saying words like those He said over Jairus' daughter: "Little girl, I say to you get up!" (Mark. 5:41), and He wants to say them over your children too.

---

1. Charles Swindoll, *Growing Wise in Family* (Hodder and Stoughton: London, 1991), p. 69.

8 WHEN THE CHURCH GETS INTO A STEW

2 Kings 4:38-44

We move now from the megamiracle of raising a dead boy to life, to two lesser-known events in the incident-strewn landscape of the fascinating and colorful ministry of Elisha.

What the world most needs to see is God's grace—His power in action to save, heal, redeem, and restore His broken world. You cannot give away grace until you have first received it. It follows that we will very likely be recruited into an extensive training program in both the receiving of God's grace and the happy experience of passing it on to others. It would be a mistake to think that this will amount to the heavenly equivalent of a pleasure cruise in the Mediterranean Sea. Grace comes to the desperate and the needy, to people in trouble. Brace yourself! We are headed for situations where grace will be much needed. The church is a battleship not a cruise-liner and battleships head for war zones not pleasure zones.

Grace will put you in some nasty predicaments

Of course we would all prefer a ministry in sun-soaked Majorca to one in famine-stricken Ethiopia, yet we may be most needed in the latter rather than the former. The backdrop to these incidents is in verse 38: "Elisha returned to Gilgal and there was famine in that region."

From this stark statement we deduce one rather unpleasant fact. God frequently places his servants (and this includes you) in circumstances of difficulty and deprivation. Of course, this was no surprise to Elisha. We have already seen him dealing with a polluted water supply at Jericho, the crippling poverty of a widow in the same region, and the terrible smell of death itself at a home in Shunem. It's almost as though the Lord said, "Very good, he's doing so well. Now what shall we expose him to next? I know! Famine!" And so, returning home to Gilgal for what he may have thought would be a well-earned break with the lads from the Bible college, Elisha walked straight into grain shortages, empty bellies, and confounded trainees, who didn't even know how to improvise properly. In short, he walked into a mess.

As we have seen, famine is one of the manifestations of the judgment of God (along with war, disease, pestilence, and religious apostasy, or error). The servants of God are not promised rapture out of trouble. All previous generations of Christians, up to and including our own, have experienced tribulation. Try telling the house churches of China, the martyrs in the Sudan, the believers in Uganda, or the people of God in Iran that they will not go through the Great Tribulation—as far as they are concerned they are in it!

God brings us there for two reasons: for our own sake, and for the sake of others—so that we may personally experience His grace, and in turn pass it on to others who need it. It's simple: we get into a fix, and then God shows us how to minister His anointing in that fix. In the course of doing that we make two surprising discoveries: God always protects, and God always provides. Grasp these two truths and you are well on your way to being prophetic in your witness for God.

This is the reason why God places us in some rather nasty predicaments from time to time. Trials, hardships, opposition, and set-backs are permitted in order to test your faith and bring out the gold.

> Consider it pure joy, my brothers, whenever you face trials of many kinds, because you know that the testing of your faith develops perseverance (James 1:2-3).

> Now for a little while you may have had to suffer grief in all kinds of trials. These have come so that your faith—of greater worth than gold, which perishes even though refined by fire—may be proved genuine and may result in praise, glory and honor when Jesus Christ is revealed (1 Pet. 1:6-7).

Grace seems to be most gratefully received and most generously passed on during trials. As somebody once put it, "Faith needs a catastrophe to walk on."

Here in Gilgal, a hundred or so trainee prophets needed to be taught a few extracurricular lessons. They needed to see some special demonstrations that God will protect and that God will provide. We do too. There will be many times when, in carrying out the will of God, we will find ourselves in danger, shortage, and want. We don't relish the thought of facing "famine or nakedness or danger or sword" (Rom. 8:35), and so God in His grace takes us involuntarily through these nasty predicaments. Sometimes the church of God gets into a very nasty stew.

Grace will give you some new priorities

The world can understand the "natural" reaction to such difficulties. It can accommodate easily our depression, complaints, anxiety, and despair. What the world cannot cope with, however, is the "supernatural" reaction of peace, trust, confidence, and perseverance in duty. In hard times there will be something inexplicable at the level of nature about the lives of believers. In any climate of economic deprivation and shortages, the natural reaction is predictable—it is selfishness and covetousness. As the late Francis Schaeffer expressed it, the priorities of a materialistic culture are "personal peace and affluence," (i.e. get all you can, can all you get). It is fascinating to see the generosity of Elisha and also that of the anonymous visitor to the college from Baal Shalishah.

> While the company of the prophets was meeting with him, he [Elisha] said to his servant, "Put on the large pot and cook some stew for these men . . . ." A man came from Baal Shalishah, bringing the man of God twenty loaves of barley bread baked from the first ripe grain, along with some heads of new grain (2 Kings 4:38, 42).

That was very generous of him, but note Elisha's spontaneous response, " 'Give it to the people to eat,' Elisha said" (v 42). Grace will make you generous. The prophetic company of saints which God is raising up in these last days will be marked by the same generosity we see here. The future of the church is not to be holed up in some survivalist fortress squatting on a stockpile of food and weapons, even if there are some who maintain that this is the Christian response to the predicted breakdown in Western economies. Our role is to give away generously all that God has first given to us.

It would have been perfectly understandable if Elisha and the man from Baal Shalishah had not acted in this way. After all, times were hard. There was a famine and Elisha could have reasoned, "I planted that vegetable garden for just such a time as this. I'm not obliged to share it. I'll wait until the economic climate is easier, until interest rates are lower and inflation is properly under control.

Maybe then prices will be lower for everyone at the supermarkets and my garden can stay intact!" Some Christians talk like this. "I'll wait until I'm no longer on a student grant and I'm earning before I show hospitality . . . I'll see the kids off our hands before we open our home to the homeless . . . It would be a different story if the wife was earning, we could afford to give more." Resources were scarce for Elisha, yet here he is twice offering to feed the students from the Bible college.

Again it required real effort. The man from Baal Shalishah lived in a village near Mount Ephraim, some distance from Gilgal. It was a mark of his true spirituality that he delivered the bread to Elisha. The "firstfruits" of a crop normally had to go to the house of God (Lev. 23:20) for the benefit of the priests (Num. 18:8-13). This man boycotted the apostate official religious center and the corrupt priests in Jerusalem, and personally delivered his gifts where he knew they would do the most good. The effort paid off, and we, too, must learn to channel our material resources and money to ministries where the truth is upheld and freely proclaimed. Let's not do the Devil's work for him by starving out God's prophetic word and effectively silencing His messengers for lack of funds.

Elisha could have argued that the loaves were a gift and therefore his to keep and not to give away. We tend to view any sudden increase in personal prosperity (pay rise, tax refund, inheritance, or financial gift) as a personal possession meant for our own exclusive use. Much so-called "prosperity teaching" runs to seed at this point. The prosperity terminates with the recipient and is only rarely given away. Such people have lost sight of the reason why God has prospered them. "And God is able to make all grace abound to you, so that in all things at all times, having all that you need, you will abound in every good work" (2 Cor. 9:8). God gives us more so that we will have more to give.

So if you've recently received promotion at work or prospered in business, or if you've been awarded a substantial raise and things are a lot easier for you now, do you remember what you pictured yourself doing for God's kingdom if He ever prospered you? Why not match the desire with action? Can God trust you with prosperity or will covetousness and selfishness crowd out your plans to give some of it away? If that much-needed raise or bonus has come, have you, at last, seriously started tithing? Ron Blue, a Christian financial counselor, has calculated that "if all Christians were reduced to a welfare check from Social Security and they tithed on that amount, the church overall would double its receipts."

Grace links us with God's supply line, and as such we are meant to traffic in all that He gives us so that many deserving causes and worthy people can be blessed by the supplies relayed both by ourselves and countless others like us.

Grace will give you protection

> Elisha returned to Gilgal and there was a famine in that region. While the company of the prophets was meeting with him, he said to his servant, "Put on the large pot and cook some stew for these men."
>
> One of them went out into the fields to gather herbs and found a wild vine. He gathered some of its gourds and filled the fold of his cloak. When he returned, he cut them up into the pot of stew, though no one knew what they were. The stew was poured out for the men, but as they began to eat it, they cried out, "O man of God, there is death in the pot!" And they could not eat it.
>
> Elisha said, "Get some flour." He put it into the pot and said, "Serve it to the people to eat." And there was nothing harmful in the pot (2 Kings 4:38-41).

This is a reminder that we live in a sin-cursed world. God told Adam, "Cursed is the ground because of you" (Gen. 3:17). The evidence is everywhere: weeds, thorns, noxious plants, and toxic substances. Sometimes these dangers lurk under the guise of attractive harmlessness and beautiful innocence, but more frequently (thank God) harmful fruit, flowers, and leaves look, smell, and taste awful—they clearly give a signal *"Warning*: I am best avoided if you wish to stay well."

Many Bible students and preachers, unlike their master Jesus, are commonly very impractical men. Giving themselves to the world of ideas, they sometimes neglect the development of practical and manual skills—such as cooking. Among those one hundred "rookie" prophets, they couldn't find one cook. Elisha entrusted the job to his servant Gehazi, but one of those students, eager to play Martha Stewart or the Frugal Gourmet to his associates, went off to find a few exotic ingredients to help spice up what on his reckoning would have been a fairly bland stew. The students' premature expedition into the master chef cooking class nearly proved disastrous.

Commentators suggest that the wild gourds were probably a type of cucumber called a colloquinth, which looks harmless enough but has a bitter noxious taste indicating that it is poisonous. We can learn a few things from this accident which nearly wiped out the Gilgal school of the prophets.

1. It was brought about through acting without authorization

Initiative is one thing, but proud independent action is another. Elisha hadn't commanded this and an ignorant, independent spirit can endanger other people's lives. It was carried out with good intentions, but good intentions can be very dangerous if we have no word from God to authorize what we do. All heresy begins in this way.

2. It exposed the ignorance of others

Not only was the cook fooled by the gourds, so was everybody else. "No one knew what it was," so they all examined these cute little cucumbers; in they went anyway, passing inspection on the basis of color and appearance alone. Besides there were lots of them and they were very hungry. We need discernment today. Discernment is the ability to shorten the gap between being presented with toxins and recognizing their deadly nature.

3. It was discovered only through painful experience

It was only after they ate, tasted, and felt (possibly a few stomach cramps set in) that they became wise to their danger. Yet we can thank God that though the discovery was made late, it was not too late. Let's learn to test all things (1 Thes. 5:2) especially the words of men. "Hear my words, you wise men; listen to me, you men of learning. For the ear tests words as the tongue tastes food" (Job 34:2-3).

By contrast, Elisha was sensitive to the Holy Spirit. He leaped into action, the action of a man who knows how to apply the antidote. And yet this was a very strange antidote. "Get some flour" (v 41). He simply threw in some meal. There is no scientific basis for that action. It was an action dictated by the sovereign Spirit of God. God's Elisha must know how to apply the supernatural remedy to many cases of toxic poisoning threatening the church today. For example:

The narcotic of false teaching (2 Tim. 2:17)

This numbs its victims to reality and dulls them to any sense of urgency. Fundamental teachings like the deity of Christ, the atoning death of Christ, salvation by faith alone, the reality of heaven and hell, and the supernatural power of God at work today are all either distorted or denied. The antidote is truth.

The irritant of bitterness (Heb. 12:15)

Unforgiveness will cause you to burn inside, choke on good

food, withdraw from company, and it may even eat away at your internal organs. The antidote is forgiveness, both given and received.

The corrosive of moral failure

Examples of this include David's adultery, Ananias and Sapphira's deceit, or Peter's cowardly denial of Jesus (2 Sam. 11; Acts 5; Luke 22:54-62). The antidote is genuine repentance.

The deliriant of pride

We have an example in 3 John. Diotrephes "loved the pre-eminence"; he was a man with the lust for power and position who shunned authority and what he perceived as competitors in his life. The antidote is servanthood and humility.

The convulsant of demonic wisdom

In James 3:14-16 there is a devilish "wisdom" which produces only quarreling, envy, and evil practices—spasms of temper tantrums, outbursts of noisy rage, and fits of slander and criticism. The antidote is the wisdom from above which comes by the renewal of the Holy Spirit.

The company of the prophets still had to eat the stew. This in itself was an act of faith for they had to trust Elisha's word and risk colic (or worse) all over again. Any anxiety was misplaced however, for God backed up the actions of His chosen man and "there was nothing harmful in the pot."

Thank God for His preventive and curative, often nick-of-time protection.

Grace will give you needed provision

A man came from Baal Shalishah, bringing the man of God twenty loaves of barley bread baked from the first ripe grain, along with some heads of new grain. "Give it to the people to eat," Elisha said.

"How can I set this before a hundred men?" his servant asked. But Elisha answered, "Give it to the people to eat. For this is what the LORD says: 'They will eat and have some left over.' " Then he set it before them, and they ate and had some left over, according to the word of the LORD (2 Kings 4:42-44).

The tasty and wholesome pot of stew was soon consumed, but the famine continued. Yet as we have seen, this miracle did not exhaust God's resources in meeting the nutritional needs of His choice servants. An anonymous benefactor arrived from Baal Shalishah with twenty loaves of barley bread. This was marvelous, but it was not enough. And yet it was provision that came just at the right time, and from unexpected quarters. Former generations of believers have experienced a great deal of God's dealings along these lines.

In the nineteenth century, Dr. Barnardo conceived the idea of putting London's homeless waifs and stray children into the safety and security of small cottages where they could be loved and cared for. Close friends tried to dissuade Barnardo on the grounds that this was a pointless and well-nigh crazy idea. Barnardo wavered, unsure whether or not this was God's will.

At that time he attended a conference in Oxford, and settled in to a small hotel in the town. He had barely begun to unpack his cases when a knock came at his door. Barnardo opened the door to see a total stranger staring him in the face. The stranger said, "Dr. Barnardo?"

"Yes?" Barnardo replied.

The stranger said, "You are thinking of building a little village for orphan girls at Ilford, are you not?"

"Yes," the doctor admitted.

"Well, put me down for the first cottage," said his visitor, placing a check for a large amount of money in Barnardo's hands, and promptly left, closing the door with a gentle click. The rest is history.

This generation needs to see similar faith ventures, possibly even on a grander scale. As we watch Elisha take what he has and move out in trust to impart what he does not yet have, we see something of the dynamics of faith. Faith is listed as one of the gifts of the Spirit in 1 Corinthians 12:9. It is a divinely given certainty that the impossible will happen. There are three elements in its development.

1. It is conceived as a persuasion or certainty in the heart.
2. It is gestated by confession with the mouth.
3. It is born by obedient action in accord with what God has directed to do.

Elisha received the donation of twenty loaves and instantly the certainty came to his mind that God would multiply them. He spoke out this conviction. "Give it to the people to eat, for this is what the LORD says: 'They will eat and have some left over'" (v 43). In spite of the skeptical questioning of his servant Gehazi, Elisha remained persuaded that what he had said would truly happen. It takes faith to give away at God's prompting that which is just sufficient for your own personal needs and perhaps those of your own immediate dependents, and those alone.

God honored this by a miraculous multiplication. The loaves multiplied even as they were set before the hungry prophets. God can multiply our resources in ways which we find inexplicable at the natural level.

It is significant that both of these miracles were connected with food. It is important that we too expect and look for the supernatural activity of God even in connection with a simple daily activity like eating. This is one reason why we say grace before meals. By praying in this way Paul says, " . . . everything God created is good, and nothing is to be rejected if it is received with thanksgiving, because it is consecrated by the word of God and prayer" (1 Tim. 4:4-5). Such praying may undo the harm of any hidden toxins in the food and also extend its virtues by enabling whatever nutritional value it contains to be used efficiently for the health and well-being of our bodies.

And so we take note that God's provision is not confined to Cadillacs and caviar alone (though some televangelists seem to think it is), rather that provision may entail nothing more impressive than cucumber stew and a stack of plain barley loaves. The point is, when God provides in response to our faith, His supply will always be all that we personally need with enough to spare for others.

But, in order to see that, you may have to get into a stew first.

9 FOR THE FIRST TIME IN YOUR LIFE FEEL REALLY CLEAN

2 Kings 5:1-19

It has been estimated that between 20 percent and 30 percent of the British population are "lepers."

This may seem to be an outrageous statement to some. "Leprosy" is something we associate with hideous photographs of the deformed victims of a gruesome complaint which afflicts unfortunate people in parts of the East or in Africa. However, what we commonly call "leprosy", or Hansen's disease, was as little known in Palestine in pre-Christian times as it is in modern Britain today. The term "leprosy" follows the Greek word *lepra* (scale) which in turn translates the Hebrew word *tsara'at*. In its most basic meaning it denotes "serious skin disease."

In his outstanding commentary on Leviticus,[1] Gordon Wenham has a masterly discussion of the section which deals with this (Leviticus 13 and 14), in which he establishes conclusively that it is most unlikely that the Bible has in mind anything like Hansen's disease in its references to leprosy. More likely, the term applies to several diseases which cause the skin to flake off, giving a white or snowy appearance—hence the Greek translation *lepra*, which refers to this scaliness on the complexion of victims of these kinds of diseases. He makes the point that the diseases discussed as "unclean" in Leviticus 13-14 all have four features in common: "they discolor the surface, affect only a part of an object, not its totality, are more than superficial and they are usually spreading." He adds, "These symptoms are clearly abnormal, and by disfiguring the appearance of man and his works, destroy the wholeness that ought to characterize the creation. For this reason these diseases are pronounced unclean."[2] Wenham then cites the opinions of various medical experts who equate biblical "leprosy" with such fairly common complaints as psoriasis, eczema, favus, and leucoderma, all of which are chronic conditions, notoriously difficult to treat, and in some cases there is no known cure even to this day.

My home encyclopedia of medical matters has an article on "The Skin and Connective Tissue," in which the author Herbert John Spoor discusses skin diseases in general (including the four listed above) along with those which are bacterial, viral, fungal, parasitic, and environmental in origin. The list is scary and includes: acne, rosacea, lichen planus, pemphigus, alopecia, erysipelas, boils and carbuncles, impetigo, shingles, herpes simplex, warts, pityriasis, ringworm, athlete's foot, scabies, frostbite, chilblains, and other afflictions such as dandruff and the much more serious lupus erythematosus and scleroderma.[3]

Have you contracted leprosy?

I think you'll agree that most of the population have suffered from one or more of these diseases at one time or another, and that our statement that perhaps 20 percent to 30 percent of the population may be "leprous" at any one time, could be an under- rather than an over-estimation of the facts.

The next episode in Elisha's illustrious career is the healing of the Syrian leper, Naaman. When we realize just how common skin diseases actually are, and when we become aware of how disfiguring and socially embarrassing they can be to their victims, we might well feel a more than usual interest in the plight of Naaman. If we then bear in mind the emotional, psychological and behavioral factors involved in some of these skin diseases it becomes easy to see how the biblical category of "uncleanness," while it may include concepts of infection (though the ancient world knew nothing of bacteria or viruses), certainly carries the idea of "disfiguring the appearance of man" and thus "destroying the wholeness that ought to characterize the creation." In the Bible, leprosy is a vivid visible metaphor for sin and all of its gruesome effects upon men and women made in God's image.

To be healed of leprosy was therefore not only a miracle, but an event of profound significance and a cause for unrestrained celebration, for not only have the ugly symptoms been removed, but also the emotional effects have been dealt with at the same time. As with any abnormality, the inner distress it brings may be more difficult to deal with than the outer affliction. We are body-soul entities, and that is why "leprosy" stands in the Bible as an outstanding illustration of the psychosomatic effects of sin. The whole person is affected.

It would be wrong to read a story like this and simply spiritualize its details while losing sight of the fact that this skin disease (whatever it was) was totally healed. This gives hope for sufferers today: God's power is still operative to heal skin diseases. Jamie Buckingham tells the remarkable story of a four-year-old boy, Troy Mitchell, who was totally healed of eczema in one of Kathryn Kuhlman's healing services in 1969. He says, "Troy's skin was covered with large, running sores, caked over with scabs and oozing fluid. Besides this, every place skin touched skin—under his chin, his armpits, his elbows, groins, knees and in between his toes and fingers—there was an itching, burning inflammation with crusted and cracked lesions." Troy's family drove five hundred miles to one of Kathryn Kuhlman's meetings in Pittsburgh. Midway through the service Miss Kuhlman announced, "Someone is being healed of eczema." No one responded. Ten minutes later Kathryn interrupted proceedings by saying, "I'm going to have to stop the service, someone in this sanctuary is grieving the Holy Spirit."

One of Kathryn's assistants identified the row in which young Troy and his family were seated and approached his father, forcing him to divulge his little boy's need. Suddenly, Troy's mother Sharon stood and in excited expectation reached over and pulled Troy's shirt over his head. Buckingham describes what happened. "Every sore on his body—every lesion, every oozing crack in the skin—was healed. The scabs had turned to powder, and as the shirt slipped off his back they dusted to the floor. . . . Grant (the boy's father) reached over and touched the place where an especially bad, draining sore had been on his left arm. The skin was now whole, healthy. Every part of his body was clean."[4]

There are records of many such incidents of healing in the ministries of those who pray for the sick on a regular basis.[5]

The story of Naaman is one of the most powerful Old Testament anticipations of the power of the Gospel on record. It vividly describes all the essentials of repentance and renewal which take place when anyone appropriates God's remedy for sin, provided for us in Christ. We will follow the story and pick up the details.

Like many non-Christians he came to see his need of God

> Now Naaman was commander of the army of the king of Aram [Syria]. He was a great man in the sight of his master and highly regarded, because through him the LORD had given victory to Aram. He was a valiant soldier, but he had leprosy (2 Kings 5:1).

Many people in our Western culture can identify with Naaman in many respects. God is on the periphery of their lives, and He is considered an irrelevance to their daily living perhaps for exactly the same reasons. Naaman had prospered. Having climbed the ranks in the Syrian army, he had a top post and all the rewards which went with it. His prominence had ensured a position in the highest echelons of Syrian society. He was powerful and highly successful in one of the most precarious careers in the ancient world. He had not only survived many close-run battles, he had so far succeeded in them all.

Interestingly, this success is attributed to Yahweh, the God of Israel. God is the one who brings all men and women into positions of power and authority. God controls the lives and destinies of men and of nations, even pagan nations. Unbelievers do not know how much they owe to God for their position and influence. Money, fame, and power in themselves are notoriously dissatisfying—they are incapable of meeting the deepest needs of man. The American billionaire Howard Hughes lived like a hermit because of his deep paranoia. Ex-Beatle John Lennon was unable to enjoy his wealth and fame because of his many fears. Joseph Stalin took elaborate precautions to elude possible assassins. Money, fame, and power all proved inadequate for these men.

The "but" in each of our lives

Naaman, too, had his problems. The Bible sums them up in one curt sentence: "But . . . he had leprosy." This was a factor which seemed to negate the catalog of achievements listed above this bald statement. There is a "but" in every success story as well as in every character. In the ancient world this would have been like saying of some prominent actor, financier, or politician, "But he had AIDS," for leprosy carried something of the stigma, horror, and fear of contact or contagion which AIDS carries today.

Humanly speaking, it was incurable, frequently loathsome in appearance, wasting, ugly, and defiling. And although leprosy was not fatal, it amounted to a kind of "living death" because of the isolation and social deprivation it inevitably entailed for its victims. An ancient law in Israel sums up the feelings of horror and disgust which leprosy provoked in those closest to the sufferer:

> The person with such an infectious disease must wear torn clothes, let his hair be unkempt, cover the lower part of his face and cry out, "Unclean! Unclean!" As long as he has the infection he remains unclean. He must live alone, he must live outside the camp (Lev. 13:45-46).

I am not suggesting that Naaman came under the administration of this law, which was valid only within the borders of Israel itself, yet it is reasonable to conclude that something like its designed effect to quarantine the leper would undoubtedly have operated, at least to some degree, even in pagan Syria.

No amount of law could even begin to change Naaman's pitiable plight. It was not legislation, education, or reformation that he needed, and yet it is remarkable how many superficial remedies for the human condition are advocated by intelligent people today. Men who live in a prison of their own hurts wax eloquent on the nature of true freedom, and others who lie in the cemetery of their own failures dare to tell the rest of us how to live. In the United Kingdom not long ago the Conservative government under the leadership of Prime Minister John Major launched a "Back to Basics" campaign with emphasis on 'family values', in order to call the nation to return to elementary standards of morality and decency, particularly in areas like sexual conduct, honesty in speech, and respect for authority. Coinciding with this campaign came the shocking media coverage of the private lives of many prominent Conservative MPs, exposing their clandestine affairs, adulterous relationships, and dishonest dealings. All very embarrassing I'm sure, but highlighting again the fact that "the heart of the human problem is the problem of the human heart," and this needs more than the superficial application of the Band-Aid of mere words in order for it to be cured. The human condition is leprous, and whatever else may be said in our favor concerning our personalities, talents, abilities, and achievements, we all need a radical and lasting remedy for the deeper concerns of our defilement, fears, rebellion, and pride.

Like many non-Christians he came to hear a word from God

> Now bands from Aram had gone out and had taken captive a young girl from Israel, and she served Naaman's wife. She said to her mistress, "If only my master would see the prophet who is in Samaria! He would cure him of his leprosy" (2 Kings 5:2-3).

God usually sends sin's victims news of a remedy through the agency of personal witness. The witness in this case was a girl, probably no older than a teenager, a young prisoner of war kidnapped during a Syrian border raid into Israel some time beforehand and seconded by Naaman as one of his own household servants. In other words, a most unlikely evangelist.

God does not always protect His people from harm or disappointment, but He always protects them in it. We have only to use a little imagination to sense the distress this girl would have felt as she was snatched by the fierce and warlike Syrian raiding party. Then there was the sense of loss and grief she must have experienced as she was abducted from her family to a strange land in order to make a new home with an alien people. There is not a hint that she gave way to bitterness or self-pity. On the contrary, the girl seems to have sensed instinctively in her heart the truth stated by Paul centuries later in Romans 8:28, "And we know that in all things God works for the good of those who love him, who have been called according to his purpose." Her kidnapping had been an unqualified evil, but like Joseph she knew that "God intended it for good" (Gen. 50:20).

Two things stand out prominently in the life of this unnamed Hebrew housemaid. First, she expressed a genuine love for people. She was an unwilling captive in Naaman's household yet she could not bear to see her master suffer. She did not return a curse but only blessing to her heartless captors. Have you got irritating neighbors or an irate boss at work? Try to find out what it is that hurts them, and then you may feel differently toward them.

Second, she evidenced a genuine faith in God. Referring Naaman to Elisha she said, "He would cure him of his leprosy." She knew there was a remedy available and she commended it in the simplest possible words. Simple and accurate testimony spoken with sincere care can be very powerful in triggering the chain reaction which brings people to God. Keep on speaking—words are one of our greatest weapons. One word of truth can change a person's life.

Like many non-Christians he thought he could bargain with God

> Naaman went to his master and told him what the girl from Israel had said. "By all means, go," the king of Aram replied. "I will send a letter to the king of Israel." So Naaman left, taking with him ten talents of silver, six thousand shekels of gold

and ten sets of clothing. The letter that he took to the king of Israel read: "With this letter I am sending my servant Naaman to you so that you may cure him of his leprosy" (2 Kings 5:4-6).

The man who had levered his way to the top by the force of his personality and the weight of his talents also thought that he had leverage with God. Naaman had become painfully aware of his incurable need. He had been pointed very clearly in the right direction for a miraculous cure. Yet he still walks in the false thinking and deep-seated pride which thinks it has something to contribute, something to bargain with. Two common fallacies surface in his response to the housemaid's witness.

1. He thought he could "name-drop" for salvation

He sincerely believed that a reference or letter from the Aramean king would present impressive credentials to Elisha and even influence Elisha's God. The assumption here was that the king of Israel could command his prophets, just as the king of Aram could order the prophets of Rimmon in the Syrian capital. Someone isn't thinking straight here. The Jewish maid spoke of a prophet, but they were now looking to a king for help. This was totally mistaken. You can be both sincere and sincerely wrong at the same time. Many people talk as if details do not matter in the question of salvation; they think it is sincerity alone which counts. "After all," they say, "one religion is as good as another." They argue that it is not a case of what you know, but whom you know. "My father's a pastor," "My uncle's a priest," "I've actually touched the Pope," "I'm a great admirer of Billy Graham. I deeply respect his religious faith." It is a form of salvation by proxy, a second-hand religion where the needy are pleased to receive someone else's cast-off and hand-me-down spiritual experiences, but have no direct dealings with God for themselves. They believe that God can be coerced into blessing them as long as they mention the right names.

Naaman, at this point, clearly thought that he could manipulate God's prophet. His plan was to persuade his sovereign to "lean on" the king of Israel, who in turn might pressure his "mumbo-jumbo" prophet to come up with the goods. The truth is that God is at nobody's beck and call, and no state ruler can dictate to the independence of a prophet of Yahweh, quite simply because no earthly king can dictate to the King of kings. Naaman had to find this out.

2. He thought he could pay for salvation

It was an impressive trove of treasure which Naaman loaded into his caravan, "ten talents of silver, six thousand shekels of gold and ten sets of clothing" (v 5b). He was clearly under the impression that Elisha, and possibly Elisha's God, could either be bribed or bought off. The fact remains that they can't. If they could be bought and this was the price, then most of us simply could not afford it. Many people would like to be healed, but they want to "go private" and not stand in line at the local hospital, waiting at the emergency room with all the other riffraff until the Divine Physician will see them. But the gospel reduces millionaires to the same level as a pauper on the streets. Skin-deep a man may be very wealthy and important, but deep down he is as impoverished as the rest of us and in need of the same God-given hope and help which comes free of charge to all. It is irrelevant what man has to offer; the important thing is what he needs to receive. God will treat the president in exactly the same way as he treats the president's chauffeur. Riches (or the lack of them) do not feature in the equation, for God cannot be bought. Some things are worth more than money; salvation is one of them. Salvation is free because it was purchased with the most precious substance in the universe—the blood of God's Son; God's blood (Acts 20:28).

God was about to show Naaman that salvation is a gift.

Like many non-Christians he took offense at God's actions

> As soon as the king of Israel read the letter, he tore his robes and said, "Am I God? Can I kill and bring back to life? Why does this fellow send someone to me to be cured of his leprosy? See how he is trying to pick a quarrel with me!" When Elisha the man of God heard that the king of Israel had torn his robes, he sent him this message: "Why have you torn your robes? Have the man come to me and he will know that there is a prophet in Israel." So Naaman went with his horses and chariots and stopped at the door of Elisha's house. Elisha sent a messenger to say to him, "Go wash yourself seven times in the Jordan, and your flesh will be restored and you will be cleansed."
>
> But Naaman went away angry and said, "I thought that he would surely come out to me and stand and call on the name of the LORD his God, wave his hand over the spot and cure me of my leprosy. Are not Abana and Pharpar, the rivers of Damascus, better than any of the waters of Israel? Couldn't I wash in them and be cleansed?" So he turned and went off in a rage (2 Kings 5:7-12).

Upon arrival in Israel, the Syrian expeditionary force really disturbed the king of Israel, who saw the whole enterprise as a provocation, an attempt to break the uneasy peace between the two nations and to pick a quarrel that would precipitate further hostilities. At least the king knew that he could not do God's job for him, but he did not know where to turn for an answer. Fortunately Elisha took the initiative and upon hearing of Joram's distress he invited the Syrian general to come straight to his residence in Gilgal.

Just picture the next scene as Naaman's horses and chariots sweep around in an impressive swirl of billowing dust and screeching wheels at the threshold of Elisha's humble dwelling. This man is still trying to impress God. He does not ride alone to see the prophet, but instead he mounts a show, the sheer scale of which is designed to tell Elisha that a very important visitor has arrived; one of the world's "big shots" has come to church this morning and everybody must know it. Have you seen them? First time in church they chew gum, make a noise, leer sarcastically, look bored, huff angrily during the worship, look daggers at the preacher during the sermon, and generally let us know by their defiant folded arms and threatening glances that they are not about to back down and let God be God in their lives. People like this need to be cut down to size.

Cutting the proud down to size

I recall reading in the biography of Brownlow North (a Scottish evangelist of the last century) that on one occasion when he was preaching at a public rally, a well-educated and arrogant young man came to speak with him after the message had been delivered. He said, "I've heard you preach quite often and I do not care for either you or your preaching. Unless you can tell me why God permitted sin in the world, I can't even begin to give credence to what you have to say."

North sized up his cocky interrogator and then replied, "God permitted sin to enter the world because He chose to do so, and if you continue to question and criticize God's dealings, vainly puffed up in your carnal mind as you are, wanting to be wiser than what

God has written, then I'll tell you something more that God will choose to do ... He will some day choose to put you in hell!"

Another of my favorite stories concerns another great evangelist of that era, the famous Chicago revivalist, D. L. Moody. Moody was conducting a series of meetings in central London in the 1880s, and each night's attendance grew larger and larger. One night Moody climbed the platform steps to preach and as he did so a stranger rushed to him and pressed an envelope into his hand. During the introductions Moody tore open the envelope and read the note inside. It had one word written upon it. In bold capitals it simply said, "FOOL!" Moody walked to the podium. He said, "I have received many letters from correspondents in the past who have written me a note but failed to add their signature ... this is the first time I have ever received a signature but no letter!" He then changed his text to Psalm 14:1: "The fool says in his heart, 'There is no God!' " and preached a stunning address on the folly and blindness of atheism and received scores of converts into God's kingdom.

Elisha belonged to the same school of the prophets. The Lord assigned him to cut this proud Syrian down to size. Elisha could see the general's inflated sense of self-importance and spiritual pride, so, not even stepping out to speak personally with Naaman, he sent word via a messenger with instructions for Naaman to dip seven times in the River Jordan, accompanied by the promise that this action would clean him of his leprosy. This was the method designated to show Naaman that only the power of God could heal him.

Naaman drove off in a huff. To say the least, he was quite miffed that God did not fit into his expectations. Every sinner has his own idea of how God should work: "I thought that he would surely come to me and stand and call on the name of the Lord his God, wave his hand over the spot and cure me of my leprosy." If I went to my doctor with a broken leg and told him what to do with his instruments, forceps, syringes, sutures, and plaster, I would be giving him the clear impression, "I could do this better myself." No doctor would submit to the patient's advice in this way, and neither will God, when He imparts healing for our greatest ills.

In short, Naaman did not like God's man, God's message, or God's method.

The call to be faithful not popular

So what is the church to do? Can we become what we are not, speak forth what we have not and act in ways we dare not, simply to impress the pride and arrogance of worldly men? God has not left that option open to us. We are God's men and women first, and our prophetic responsibility is to represent accurately something of His being, His heart and His ways before the eyes of a sometimes proud and insolent world. In Elisha's case there was no authorization for him to engage in showy prayer or magical benediction; he wasn't told to engage in a mystical incantation or to perform a sacred ceremony. He was told to talk simply and to talk straight to Naaman: "Go and take a public, prolonged, and very embarrassing dip in the silted waters of the Jordan River. It's so simple. You'll go in dirty and you'll come out clean. God bless you. Next please!"

Naaman sounds like a Texan. "Are not Abana and Pharpar, the rivers of Damascus, better than any of the waters of Israel?" "Listen, partner, back home we've got irrigation ditches bigger, faster, cleaner, and more effective than this drainage ditch y'all call a river! Why, I could have stayed home and jumped in a river any time I'd wanted."

So he could have. Abana and Pharpar would have done the job had it simply been a question of dirt. But it wasn't, it was a question of disease, and only God's remedy could deal with that. And when unimpressive preachers today tell unimpressed sinners to jump into the dark red river of Jesus" blood flowing from the still open wounds He received at Calvary, then those sinners, too, react strongly and think that they know much better techniques to clean up defiled human personalities; modern techniques, tried and tested by experts—techniques which are far more relevant to the needs of late-twentieth-century men than our antiquated Gospel. But like Naaman, they are wrong. Dead wrong.

There is all the difference in the world between magic and miracle. In magic, men try to manipulate God: in miracle, God takes the initiative to show mercy to men. The former requires the right technique, but the latter simply requires trust. This necessitates a huge climb down on the part of leprous men and women because it is such an offense to their independence and pride. But if in rejecting the Gospel because it is "too simple," or "not intellectually satisfying," or "doesn't fit our religious sensitivities," you go home still eaten up by leprosy, then what good is the psychobabble of self-made religion? There are plenty of "better" rivers on offer today, plenty of religious options and spiritual experiences to be tested and tasted, but if God says, "It's the Jordan," you had better take a dip. And if God says, "It's Jesus," you had better humble yourself and take a trip—to the cross. "Salvation is found in no one else, for there is no other name under heaven given to men by which we must be saved" (Acts 4:12).

A great many people of wealth and status would like to go to heaven, but not on God's omnibus sharing the same "economy class" seats as the rest of us. Salvation comes by complying with what God actually says and not what we think we would like Him to say.

Like many non-Christians he finally surrendered to God

> Naaman's servants went to him and said, "My father, if the prophet had told you to do some great thing, would you not have done it? How much more, then, when he tells you, 'Wash and be

> cleansed!' " So he went down and dipped himself
> in the Jordan seven times, as the man of God had
> told him, and his flesh was restored and became
> clean like that of a young boy (2 Kings 5:13-14).

We last saw Naaman in a rage, storming off in a proud and fuming display of temper. Many visitors to our seeker services, missions, and crusades dismiss God's power to heal and convert them, in similar storms of wounded passion and angry reaction. This is not always a bad sign, for it is better than the shrug-of-the-shoulder apathy which greets so much preaching of the Gospel today. Naaman dismissed both the preacher and his message.

Yet God had another preacher waiting in the vestry, burning with a fresh anointing from God and a new message for the stubborn Syrian commander in chief. The message was delivered with crushing eloquence and irrefutable logic. The servant points out that if a man is prepared to do great things to achieve his desired goals, then why not stoop to do lesser things? In putting it this way, he enabled Naaman to see that the good news was not only beautifully simple, it was also simply beautiful.

Naaman crumpled. The word of his servant was the combination to the lock of his hard heart. He got down off his high horse, stripped, then dipped himself, as directed, in the muddy, sluggish stream of the River Jordan. He came to see that the most important issue here was his disease (which needed saving) not his dignity (which didn't). Capitulating in this way, he obeyed God's directive to the letter. Seven consecutive plunges must have taken faith to endure, yet as he plunged and rubbed his raised reddish patches with their silvery scales, the miracle happened! The itchy, broken lesions began to fall away from his skin to be replaced by clean, properly pigmented flesh and he was instantly made whole. This is what the power of God, mediated to us through His Son Jesus Christ, does for all who submit to its terms. These terms are so simple: come to your senses and commit your life. We call this repentance and faith.

Like all new believers he now began a new life with God

> Then Naaman and all his attendants went back to the man of God. He stood before him and said, "Now I know that there is no God in all the world except in Israel. Please accept now a gift from your servant."
>
> The prophet answered, "As surely as the LORD lives, whom I serve, I will not accept a thing." And even though Naaman urged him, he refused.
>
> "If you will not," said Naaman, "please let me, your servant, be given as much earth as a pair of mules can carry, for your servant will never again make burnt offerings and sacrifices to any other god but the LORD. But may the LORD forgive your servant for this one thing: When my master enters the temple of Rimmon to bow down and he is leaning on my arm and I bow there also—when I bow down in the temple of Rimmon, may the LORD forgive your servant for this."
>
> "Go in peace," Elisha said (2 Kings 5: 15-19).

People do not step full-grown into the Christian life. They do not in one moment unlearn all of the foolishness acquired over a life time. Nevertheless, four things stand out prominently in the life of this new convert to Yahweh.

1. He was prepared to go public with his faith in the Lord

He did this first by immersion in water, then by confession with the mouth (v 15a). Here was a vivid foreshadowing of New Testament baptism and the public confession that "Jesus Christ is Lord." We underestimate to our peril the critical importance of baptism in the lives of new converts. Baptism is both a bath for the dirty and a burial for the dead. It is one of the means God uses to sever completely the former links of pagans with their pagan background. It also helps to equip the new convert to be a co-belligerent with Christ in his war with the apostate empires of this world. William Willimon expresses this forcefully when he says, "Baptism stands as a visible reminder to the church that God has graciously called us for more." He cites the testimony of a Georgian Baptist believer in the former Soviet Union who said, "To be a Christian here, to be baptized, is to be motherless. When one comes out of the water, one has lost country, parents, all."[6] It's true. We can never be the same again. We arise from those waters as preachers, heralds, and ambassadors of a new order.

Naaman was inevitably set on collision course with both Aramean culture and Aramean gods by his submission to God's word, experience of God's power and immersion in the cleansing water. So too with every baptized believer today. "Believe and be baptized" is far more than an empty formula, it is a declaration of war and a call for unconditional surrender.

2. He was prepared to lay all of his resources at the Lord's disposal

In thus laying these riches at Elisha's feet, he was giving the Lord a claim to all his property. Because Elisha waived this gift in order to prevent any misunderstanding about the true basis of salvation, we cannot deduce that the Lord has no claims on our wealth, for he does. John Wesley used to ask of new converts, "Has his pocket-book been converted yet?" We cannot pay the Lord, but we can repay Him in some way, by laying all we have and are at His disposal.

3. He was prepared to become a worshiper of the Lord

He wanted to take some point of contact with the Lord back home with him to Syria so that he could re-establish fellowship with the Lord by sacrificial worship whenever possible. He showed a degree of superstition here, but his heart was good. He wanted to jettison the old gods of sensual lust, physical power, and material greed (Baal, Moloch, and Mammon) and yield himself to the service of the one true God, Yahweh—in his home, in his work, and in his worship. To want God's presence in the whole of your life is the very essence of worship.

4. He was prepared to abandon all old rivals to the Lord

He wanted to be different. This meant an end to duplicity and living for "the best of both worlds." He knew that he could not love Yahweh and bow to Rimmon at the same time. He had to go back home to a world where God was not welcome and God was not confessed. His work took him, of necessity, into Rimmon's presence, but as far as Naaman was concerned Rimmon had no further claims upon his heart or his life. Naaman would go through the motions but not really mean it. He might bow down in body but not in spirit. It's interesting that Elisha was not too perturbed about this little compromise which so troubled Naaman's conscience. "Go in peace," he said as Naaman departed. The prophet was sure that the God who had so thoroughly cleaned up Naaman's skin would have no difficulty in totally purging Naaman's heart.

Several years ago the giant soap company Procter and Gamble launched a new bar of soap into an already competitive market. It was called Zest. Within weeks it was a top-selling brand because something about the advertising slogan used to promote it really caught the public imagination. The slogan said, "For the first time in your life feel really clean."

Naaman found that the Gospel strikes that same deep chord in all of us. No doubt you found it to be so too. The moment we take the plunge into God's remedy for sin, we experience the truth of that attractive slogan.

---

1. G. J. Wenham *The Book of Leviticus* (NICOT Wm. B. Eerdmans Publishing: Grand Rapids, Michigan, 1979), pp. 189-224.

2. *Ibid,* p. 192.

3. Herbert John Spoor in *Symptoms: The Complete Home Medical Encyclopedia,* edited by Sigmund Stephen Miller (Pan Books: London, 1979) pp. 418-433.

4. Jamie Buckingham, *Daughter of Destiny: Kathryn Kuhlman—Her Story* (Logos International: Plainfield, New Jersey, 1976), pp. 138-140.

5. For example, John Wimber, *Power Evangelism* (Hodder and Stoughton: London, 1985), pp 102–103. John White, cited in Jack Deere, *Surprised by the Power of the Spirit* (Kingsway: Eastbourne, 1994), p. 20.

6. William H. Willimon, *Peculiar Speech* (Wm. B. Eerdmans Publishing Co.: Grand Rapids, 1992), pp. 100, 114.

10 THE MAN WHO LET SLIP ON REALITY

2 Kings 5:19-27

Are you a man or a mouse?

There is a legend from India concerning a mouse which was terrified of cats. A magician agreed to help him and transformed the mouse into a cat. That seemed to resolve his fears until he came face to face with a dog. He took his case to the magician who changed him this time into a dog. The mouse-turned-cat-turned-dog was very content until he met a tiger. Crippled with fear he persuaded the magician to turn him into what he now feared most and—pouff!—he became a tiger! It wasn't long, however, before he came back to the magician in his new guise as a tiger with his brand new phobia—he had met a hunter! The magician adamantly refused to help this time. He said, "I will turn you back into a mouse, for though you have the body of a tiger, you still have the heart of a mouse."

In spite of months and years of association with Elisha, his servant Gehazi remained in essence the same man—unspiritual, hard-hearted, and mercenary—the exact opposite or alter-ego of Elisha. If Elisha's ministry served to show the world that "God saves," Gehazi modeled a ministry that falsely suggested to the world that "God soaks" people for all he can get. There are too many of his breed in the church today.

The remarkable thing is that Elisha waited so long in order to deal with him. God gave Gehazi every opportunity to change. He exposed the twisted soul of Elisha's servant to many life-changing circumstances: hardships certainly, but hardships touched again and again with the miraculous power of God. The story of Gehazi is a fascinating and frightening showcase for the power of covetousness, and its ability to shrivel a man's soul, distorting his values, destroying his ministry, and eventually robbing him of his destiny. The man who was really a mouse.

He's in it for the money

Many men and women of God have faced similar temptations in our generation. They find themselves in a job where the financial rewards are low, the perks few, and where the honor they receive is very slight indeed. They silently brood on their lot, incubating a secret rivalry and resentment toward others. They begin to play little deceitful games, minor at first, but increasing in scale with each stunt that they are able to pull off successfully. They have forgotten that God is their real employer and He is the great Promoter. He is our Rewarder, indeed He is our reward.

It is a dangerous condition indeed for a servant of God to be in the grip of covetousness. Great losses are always incurred when men and women fall into this trap. Achan caused Israel to experience defeat in a crucial battle, Ananias and Sapphira forfeited their earthly lives, and Judas Iscariot lost his eternal salvation. The news media regularly reveal the shocking news that another outstanding pastor, preacher, or evangelist has fallen because of his lust for gold, girls, or glory.

Jesus did not say, "It is a little difficult to serve God and Money." He said, "You *cannot* serve both God and Money" (Matt. 6:24; Luke 16:13). None of us is immune from the seductive approaches of the lure of money. The Bible is full of examples of once-great servants of God who chose slavery to Mammon. Esau sold his birthright, Lot chose to live in Sodom, Saul forfeited his kingdom, Samson became blind and imprisoned, Solomon decayed into debauchery and excess, Demas forsook the apostle Paul, and Diotrephes isolated his ministry—because in each case these men lusted covetously after that which God had not chosen to give them. They all failed the test. Which test was that? The test God applies to each one of us: the test which will expose our motives for ministry.

This next section (2 Kings 5:20-27) tells us how Gehazi finally let slip his footing and what he lost in the terrible fall which followed.

Losing your footing on the climb to the top

God wants us to get to the top, of course—so why do so many end up at the bottom, degraded, damaged, and dying? There are four places where the aspiring people of God can slip, lose their grip, and begin the headlong plunge to disaster. They all appear in these verses.

1. You begin to see your ministry as a lucrative business

> After Naaman had traveled some distance, Gehazi, the servant of Elisha the man of God, said to himself, "My master was too easy on Naaman, this Aramean, by not accepting from him what he brought. As surely as the LORD lives, I will run after him and get something from him" (vv 19-20).

None of us is here on earth primarily to make money. You may be skillful at doing just that of course, in which case God probably wants to give you the charismatic anointing to be a giver also (Rom. 12:8). Why are we here then? Primarily we are here to do the will of God. The bonus is that in doing the will of God, the Lord will see to it that we have all our needs and expenses met while we are on His business. In Jesus' words, "But seek first his kingdom and his righteousness, and all these things will be given to you as well" (Matt. 6:33). If we lose sight of that order of priorities then we are headed for trouble.

We can read Gehazi's mind: watching Naaman's dusty trail heading north to Syria with all those pack animals loaded with riches, he could see all that lovely money just trickling through his covetous fingers. "Elisha must be a fool!" he thought. None of us likes to lose money or to give it away in large quantities.

Gehazi knew he had to act quickly. He pictured himself coming back home with a bag full of bank notes and a self-satisfied leer on his face. And why not? "Leprosy cures don't come cheap these days, do they? We deserve remuneration. Besides, Naaman can afford it." To him religion was big business, just as it is to many healing evangelists today. Bishop Hall said of Gehazi, "His heart was packed up in Naaman's suitcases and he must run after him to fetch it."

2. You begin to see people as gullible customers

My master was too easy on Naaman, this Aramean (v 20).

You can almost hear the contempt, if not the tone of racial superiority in Gehazi's voice. He had lost sight of the value of a person and of how important each individual is to God. He saw Naaman only as "this Aramean," a chicken to be plucked for the pot. It is possible to look down contemptuously upon the uneducated or the poor, and to despise those of a different class or racial origin; to look upon them as people who are there only to serve one's own personal advantage. And so the sly fox Gehazi found his way into the chicken coop with plenty to plunder and the farmer apparently a long way off.

3. You begin to see God as the "silent partner"

As surely as the LORD lives, I will run after him (v 20).

The sheer impiety and blasphemous effrontery of it all! The sacred name of Yahweh is drawn in as some kind of scheming oath to reinforce Gehazi's resolve to pull off this audacious confidence trick at Naaman's expense. This is the name Gehazi drags into the dirt in order to have a "front" for his dirty business. It is as though the living God came to be seen as a kind of senile old member of the board who doesn't even know what day of the week it is let alone what goes on in His name on a day-to-day basis. Gehazi sneers at true spirituality and uses that name in vain. He's like those religious merchandisers who put the name of Jesus on anything from pencil erasers to bumper stickers or from candles to crucifixes—anything to make a fast buck.

4. You begin to argue that the end justifies the means

> So Gehazi hurried after Naaman. When Naaman saw him running toward him, he got down from the chariot to meet him. "Is everything all right?" he asked.
>
> "Everything is all right," Gehazi answered. "My master sent me to say, 'Two young men from the company of the prophets have just come to me from the hill country of Ephraim. Please give them a talent of silver and two sets of clothing'" (vv 21-22).

And so Gehazi became a liar. He concocted this amazing story about "two sons of the prophets," implicating Elisha and making out that the man of God was both capricious and also in collusion with this evil scheme. A strange about-turn on the part of Elisha who had hours before adamantly refused any money. In lying to men like this, Gehazi was ultimately lying to God. He was a man utterly devoid of the fear of God. To him the end justified the means. A little "heavenly deception" (as the Korean cult of the "Moonies" used to call it), is surely justified if we want to line the pockets of God's chosen servants? Snooping pagans have forfeited their right to the truth, haven't they?

Bridging the credibility gap

Many choice men and women of God have lost credibility with God and with man by stumbling over these same four loose boulders. Credibility is something that may take a long time to gain, but which can be lost almost overnight. If you stand up to speak, to sing, to lead worship, to give testimony, to commend a book or perform any service people will ask three basic questions of you.

1. "Does he know what he is talking about?"—the question of *expertise*.
2. "Do I like him?"—the question of *personality*.
3. "Can I trust him?"—the question of *trustworthiness*.

All three—expertise, personality, trustworthiness—are an essential combination if men and women are to receive what we have to give or say. Together they constitute this crucial factor of credibility in our ministry. Credibility derives from the integrity and reality of our walk with God. You cannot fake it.

Gehazi acted as a sickening example of unreality. "Naaman! Everything all right? Great day, isn't it? Hot though! Say, those donkeys look like they're heavy-laden . . . you wouldn't want to lighten their load, would you? You know . . . to help out an old friend in a fix? You could give a small offering to the Bible college . . . all donations are tax deductible too. You wouldn't even miss it with all your money. Besides, you'll get your reward in heaven!"

It all sounds so implausible and hollow to our ears, and yet Naaman was completely taken in. It is easy to take people in, particularly if you pretend to be pious. But nothing could really hide Gehazi's indifference to Naaman's spiritual welfare. He was unafraid of the possibility that Naaman might see through all this and become alienated from his newly found faith. "Salvation is free," Elisha had declared. "Oh, no, it isn't!" said Gehazi.

Naaman responded magnificently, of course. "By all means, take two talents," he said. He urged Gehazi to accept them, and then tied up the two talents of silver in two bags, with two sets of clothing. I do wonder, though, whether or not he reflected upon all of this later and sighed, "Ah well, so men are men after all when it comes to money."

Prophets confront corruption

Even if Naaman remained oblivious to the true nature of the deed, Elisha did not. Gehazi returned with his plunder and the narrative continues.

> When Gehazi came to the hill, he took the things from the servants and put them away in the house. He sent the men away and they left. Then he went in and stood before his master Elisha.
>
> "Where have you been, Gehazi?" Elisha asked.
>
> "Your servant didn't go anywhere," Gehazi answered.
>
> But Elisha said to him, "Was not my spirit with you when the man got down from his chariot to meet you?" (2 Kings 5:24-26).

It was Elisha's role as a prophet of God to confront evil not only in his nation, but also in his own household. Those with similar prophetic anointing upon their lives and ministries today must openly challenge the Gehazi spirit in individuals and the church. As with Elisha, it is likely that we will encounter a brazen denial, for Gehazi responded to Elisha's question in defensiveness and with an evasive attempt at further deception.

We will all be tested in the areas of prosperity, purity, and power sooner or later. If we do fail then God may forgive us, even if the people won't. Failure in public ministry along these lines may not be final so long as the mistakes are handled properly. Suspension from ministry for some time is usually essential, as is proper accountability to others in the Lord. The failure must be confessed and restitution made. It is vital that credibility be restored.

Gehazi proved the fact that though you can fool some of the people some of the time, you cannot fool God any of the time. The gift of prophecy includes the ability to reveal the secrets of men's hearts, and God gave Elisha the supernatural ability to monitor Gehazi's actions even when he was not personally present with him. Elisha boldly challenged Gehazi, called him to repentance, and upon seeing his cold response to this word, he then pronounced judgment upon him.

F. W. Krummacher writes these words concerning Gehazi:

> The young man whose character now emerges and engages our attention, was not a neglected uncultivated being, picked from the dregs of the people. He must have received instruction from Elisha; he was his servant and companion in travel ... it can hardly be doubted that Elisha entertained high hopes respecting this spirited and evidently gifted young man.

But Gehazi lost it all. A fall of this kind invariably entails a great deal of loss if the way back to recovery is either neglected or declined. Gehazi missed his chance, and within the next breath Elisha sealed his doom. Gehazi may have been one of the figures in Paul's mind when he wrote,

> People who want to get rich fall into temptation and a trap and into many foolish and harmful

desires that plunge men into ruin and destruction. For the love of money is a root of all kinds of evil. Some people, eager for money, have wandered from the faith and pierced themselves with many griefs (1 Tim. 6:9-10).

What you might have to jettison on the way down
Gehazi lost four things:
1. He lost his integrity—he went downhill *morally*.
2. He lost his sense of urgency—he went downhill *emotionally*.
3. He lost his destiny—he went downhill *spiritually*.
4. He lost his vitality—he went downhill *physically*.

It is all contained in Elisha's closing words.

> "Is this the time to take money, or to accept clothes, olive groves, vineyards, flocks, herds, or menservants and maidservants? Naaman's leprosy will cling to you and to your descendants forever." Then Gehazi went from Elisha's presence and he was leprous, as white as snow (vv 26-27).

Morally we saw Gehazi fall into thieving and deceit. Emotionally the result was that this completely distorted his vision—his personal vision for his own life, and his global vision for the kingdom of God. The servant who was undoubtedly being groomed as Elisha's successor as God's seer, narrowed his vision dramatically. Elisha summed it up: it shrank only to include "clothes, olive groves, vineyards, flocks, herds ... menservants and maidservants." That was evidently all that Gehazi planned to spend his ill-gotten gains upon. These ambitions at first sight seem to be large, expansive, fulfilling, and satisfying. In fact they were a very poor trade-off. Gehazi sold out his once rich plans for a life dominated by money, fashion, property, and position. Elisha rebuked him, not because his vision was too large but because it was too small. You and I only have one life to live, and it is too valuable to be squandered frivolously on lesser goals.

Spiritually, then, Gehazi lost his destiny. This life is the only one you have—the all-important question is this: What does God want you to do with it? What is your destiny?

In the book of Esther, Mordecai thundered a challenge to his tunnel-visioned niece who was in danger of selling out to the status quo and ignoring the divinely given opportunity hanging over her life. "If you remain silent at this time, relief and deliverance for the Jews will arise from another place, but you and your father's family will perish. And who knows but that you have come to royal position for such a time as this?" (Es. 4:14). Esther rose to the challenge, but Gehazi didn't. It is as simple and as bleak as that. His story is a lesson to us. If the times really are as urgent as they appear, then "it is not the time" for us to give ourselves to lesser things and to lose our destiny.

Physically Gehazi's end was tragic. The judgment had a note of irony about it. In coveting from Naaman what he most wanted to have, namely his wealth, he received instead what he most wanted to avoid—his leprosy! Lack of wholeness on the inside would be manifested by a lack of wholeness on the outside. There is a kind of poetic justice about it all—live for things that perish and you will perish along with them.

How the mighty have fallen

One of the most tragic scenes I ever read was the account of a journalist who paid a visit to the former world heavyweight boxing champion, Muhammad Ali. Muhammad Ali (or Cassius Clay as he was once known) was world famous. His face appeared regularly on sports magazine covers, television talk shows, award ceremonies, and even at presidential dinners. He fought at sell-out fights. He had a slogan: he would "float like a butterfly and sting like a bee." And then Muhammad Ali disappeared from view. Sports writer Gary Smith eventually traced him down to his secluded private dwelling. Ali showed the reporter some old mementos in the barn adjacent to the house. There were photographs and portraits of the champion boxer, posing in his sculpted body—pictures which included the moment he held the world championship winner's belt over his head with the caption "The Thrilla in Manilla" emblazoned across it.

Then Smith noticed a very poignant thing. On the photograph of the champ were pigeon droppings dribbled in white streaks which had fallen from the birds high up in the rafters of the barn.

Ali walked over to the row of pictures, turned them face down and mumbled something. Smith asked him to repeat it. "I had the world," he said, "and it wasn't *nothin'* . . . *nothin'* . . . *now!*" and Ali pointed to the pigeon dung adorning the record of his greatest moment. The cob-webbed, bird-limed trophies and the fading, soiled pictures were all the proof one needed; visible evidence of the emptiness, fickleness, and forgetfulness of worldly fame and acclaim.

Don't repeat Gehazi's foolish choice.

Don't miss your destiny.

HAVE YOU LOST YOUR EDGE LATELY?

11

2 Kings 6:1-7

A father collected his son from junior church and asked what Bible story they had heard.

"It was about Moses and the Israelites, Dad," replied the boy. "They were trapped with the Red Sea in front of them and the Egyptian army behind."

"So what happened?" asked the father.

"Well—Moses sent some tanks back to face the Egyptians and radioed for support to some warships anchored in the gulf. While the navy bombers attacked Pharaoh's troops and chariots, helicopters airlifted the Hebrews to safety on the other shore."

Dad laughed. "Sounds a bit far-fetched to me. I don't remember that story from Sunday school."

"I know, Dad," replied his son. "But if I told you what really happened, you'd never believe it!"

There are some stories like that scattered throughout the Bible. In telling us what really happened the author never seems to be troubled about whether or not we'll believe it. The story of the floating ax-head is one of those stories. It's the kind of passage a preacher dreads if he is teaching a consecutive series. Weeks beforehand the question begins to nag, "What on earth am I going

151

to say about that?" Often the commentators give little or no help; they either ignore it or trivialize it. For example, with regard to this particular incident, one commentator explained that Elisha probably took a long straight rod like a punting pole and either (a) inserted the pole into the hole on the sunken ax-head or (b) shoved the lost implement to shallow water where it could be retrieved from the riverbank. If that is so, one is tempted to ask why this story has been recorded in the Bible at all. Perhaps to encourage thick people to use sticks to retrieve ax-heads from rivers?

But we are not entitled either to ignore or to trivialize any part of the Word of God. Our best option is to take the story at face value and to deduce what pertinent instruction we can from it. We can best deal with the passage by asking three questions which can be derived from it.

Question one: have you built for growth lately?

> The company of the prophets said to Elisha, "Look, the place where we meet with you is too small for us. Let us go to the Jordan, where each of us can get a pole; and let us build a place there for us to live." And he said, "Go." Then one of them said, "Won't you please come with your servants?" "I will," Elisha replied. And he went with them (2 Kings 6:1-4).

"The place . . . is too small." That's a good problem to have. It's a good problem for a church as its premises bulge at capacity with the numbers of people God draws in, and it's also a good problem for a Bible college to have, indicating the high incidence of men and women feeling the call of God to prepare themselves for Christian ministry.

This story, appearing as it does sandwiched between the

gloomy account of the fall of Gehazi—the man who missed his destiny—and the story of Elisha in jeopardy at the hands of the king of Aram, reminds us that blessings come in the midst of trouble. There are signs of burgeoning spiritual life even against the dark backdrop of political upheaval and spiritual declension.

Elisha's anointing inspired other aspirants for ministry to gather around him. This is inevitable. Healthy leadership reproduces itself in the lives of others, not only equipping the people of God to exemplify a prophetic lifestyle during tense times, but also birthing similar ministries. The training of other leaders becomes a high priority in the agenda of any truly prophetic movement. The last thing men and women aspire to during times of spiritual decline is to enter the Christian ministry. Conversely, the multiplication of such leadership and ministry is a sure sign of recovery and growth.

Furthermore, the fact of multiplied ministries makes building projects inevitable. Existing facilities become stretched and then totally inadequate. The work of God needs the fabric and infrastructure of facilities, buildings, houses, churches, and land to consolidate and to advance its growth even further. Sin, heresy, and unbelief shut down Bible colleges and churches; obedience, truth, and living faith maintain and open them.

Notice also that this idea came from the students themselves. Elisha was humble and teachable enough to see that the idea came from God, even though he had not thought of it. In the advance of God's kingdom existing leaders do not have a monopoly on divine initiatives and ideas. God can speak to us through anyone He chooses, and may speak from some very surprising quarters. We must value the insights of even the most unlikely people and refuse to stamp on the Spirit's prompting when they come through unusual channels.

It is noteworthy that they struck a balance between luxury and poverty. They didn't put up with old, dilapidated premises because "building projects are a waste of the Lord's money!" Nor did they mine marble, fell the cedars of Lebanon, and erect a crystal cathedral. We are to pursue excellence in what we do but refuse to squander hard-earned resources. Building projects involve great personal sacrifice and large-scale individual involvement. This project was owned by each of them in that they resolved to gather materials together: "Let us go to the Jordan, where each of us can get a pole" (v 2). Those students were not afraid of hard manual work. Everybody "mucked in" together, and everybody gave of their time, money, effort, and resources.

Spiritual growth is something we should not only expect but work for. It is the result of two factors: first, the pursuit of healthy spiritual life centered around the anointed ministry of God's Word. A combination of Word and Spirit is essential to success. The Spirit without the Word leads to fanaticism; the Word without the Spirit leads to intellectualism and cynicism. We need both. Second, there is a preparedness for hard work on the part of all. In God's kingdom there are no gains without pains.

Question two: have you experienced a stroke of "bad luck" lately?

Sometimes Christians are naive. They expect a steady state of advancement without discouragement, opposition, setback, or difficulty. This is a very simplistic view. It is the very fact of increase and blessing which draws to itself resistance and opposition. Things go wrong and many Christians tend to fall apart. They react like unbelievers do when they encounter a stroke of bad luck. Here is an example.

> They went to the Jordan and began to cut down trees. As one of them was cutting down a tree, the iron ax-head fell into the water. "Oh, my lord," he cried out, "it was borrowed!" The man of God asked, "Where did it fall?" When he showed him

the place, Elisha cut a stick and threw it there, and
made the iron float. "Lift it out," he said. Then the
man reached out his hand and took it (2 Kings
6:4b-7).

One of the students was hacking away at a rather stubborn tree
on the banks of the sluggish River Jordan. Unaware that the head
of his ax was working loose, he set to with such gusto that the iron
blade slipped from its shaft on an upward stroke, arched through
the air and landed with a "bloop" midstream in the Jordan, sinking
out of reach and out of sight in the midst of the muddy river. Worse
still, the ax had been borrowed. Doesn't it always happen with stuff
you have borrowed? My wife and I borrowed a car for one day from
a pastor, and as we drove home the axle broke! I once drove a friend
to school in his car since his leg was in plaster; we turned a corner
at some traffic lights and the front wheel fell off. Not my fault, of
course, but it looked suspiciously like it. Why do things always go
wrong when you borrow (or lend) something, especially when it's
"the Lord's work" we're about? Is it just "bad luck" or has God engineered something magnificent to emerge from all this? That
depends upon whether you walk by fate or by faith.

You can walk by fate

To put it mildly, this is less than a Christian perspective on
things. Yet many believers share a non-Christian worldview when
it comes to the crunch in their lives. Their view on the world and
some of its more bizarre happenings is governed by a kind of fatalism. Murphy's Law says "If anything can go wrong it will." A
variation on that law says that if you drop a piece of buttered toast,
it always lands buttered-side down. As bad as that sounds, there are
still people around who adamantly maintain that Murphy was an
optimist!

Ancient Greek mythology believed in the control of man's life
and destiny by the Fates. The god Pluto was king of the

Underworld, the abode of the dead. A stern and pitiless deity, he would listen neither to flattery nor prayer. From his residence in that gloomy, black underworld, he would work out his plans with the help of the three Fates, who controlled the length of people's lives.

I remember reading how Kenneth Chafin, a Christian author, used to check out books from the local library for his aging grandmother. Each time she received a novel she would always read the last chapter before she went on to start at the beginning. Puzzled, Chafin asked her why, and she replied, "Because if I don't like how the book ends why should I be bothered wasting time reading it?" The logic seems irrefutable. Many unbelievers don't like the way they perceive that the world will end. They don't like the idea of how their own small lives will end either. They conclude, "If I don't like the way life ends, then why should I be bothered living it?" From their perspective, suicide seems like a very sensible option. This issue of fatalism is not, therefore, merely a lesson in ancient history.

Our modern world is deeply marinaded with the ideas of fate and chance. Soldiers at war speak of "the bullet with your name on it." Actors are deeply superstitious. Athletes carry lucky charms on to the field in order to give themselves an edge. Does fate decide our lives in the small details as well as the total canvas? Are we doomed to face heart-rending disappointments which are cruelly dealt to us by some divine torturer? Woody Allen, the film director and humorist, summed up the choices open to fatalists in this way. "Civilization stands at the crossroads. Down one road is despondency and despair, and down the other is total annihilation. Let us pray that we choose the right road!"

If you resign yourself to fatalism then you can be sure that your resignation will be accepted. As believers, however, we have another choice. We do not walk by fate. We walk by faith.

You can walk by faith
Faith is the dynamic ingredient which enables us to invite the

living and personal God into our disasters. Faith looks beyond our troubles to the God who is bigger than all of our misfortunes. Certainly from the human perspective accidents frequently occur, and here we can define an "accident" as an "occurrence or an effect which is produced in ways unforeseen or even unrelated to the actions of the main performer." From faith's perspective, accidents change color and may be seen differently once God is brought into the picture.

The God of the Bible is a good God. He can straighten things out. He fixes things; indeed, he fixes them so well that bad things can be made to look good, they fit so well into God's plan (see Rom. 8:28). The Lord totally controls all things, as this shrieking, panic-stricken student ("There goes my grant!") was to find out.

He came to Elisha and explained the problem, and Elisha cared, because God cares. We can ask God to bring good out of "accidents," we can ask him to help us find lost things, we can invite him to show us the way out when there seems no way out (1 Cor. 10:13). Elisha responded by performing a symbolic action. He threw in "a stick" says the NIV, but the Hebrew can mean a "sapling" or even a "tree." The tree becomes a catalyst for the supernatural power of God to go to work. The tree had no inherent power of its own (neither does the oil with which we anoint the sick, the hands we lay on people's bodies, or the water in which we immerse new believers) but it became a sacrament—a physical action which has spiritual effects—when God so ordered it. God moves in supernatural power above, through and alongside this unlikely instrument.

We cannot explain what happened, only state that God made the iron to float like wood. God can turn tragedies into triumphs and disappointments into divine appointments. God can make our reverses look like a move forward, and bad luck can turn into bad news for the devil. Helen Keller spoke the truth when she said, "The world is full of suffering; it is also full of the overcoming of it." The Lord makes us "more than conquerors" in times of trouble.

Our problems matter to God, even the little ones, because little things matter to God. God colored the wings of a mayfly even though it lives for only a few hours and may never be seen by the eyes of men. John Newton, the converted slave trader, said,

> Not one concern of ours is small if we belong
> to Him,
> To teach us this the Lord of all once made the iron
> to swim.

When you are next face-to-face with a difficulty try to recall that you may well be also in line for a discovery—the discovery that God loves you and that He can make iron float; He can recover the unrecoverable and retrieve the unretrievable.

Paul Claudel expressed it like this: "Christ did not come to do away with suffering; He did not come to explain it; He came to fill it with His presence." That is why we Christians are not fatalists. We put our faith in God. Christianity is great news for everybody who loves a happy ending.

Question three: have you lost your edge lately?

This unfortunate prophet who was "jinxed with bad luck" and lost the head off a borrowed ax reminds us of the all-too-familiar scenario of Christians engaged in active ministry who somewhere along the way lose their cutting edge. They may still be going through the motions of activity and busyness for the Lord, but they are not felling any trees. In fact, they are no longer making even a dent for the Lord.

In this connection it is worth pointing out that in every case, our ministry is, like this ax, a borrowed one. It is not inherently our own, for we did not originate it or pay for it nor do we own it. Someone has entrusted it to us and may call it back, or at least call us to account for how we have used it.

The most salutary point is surely the fact that we can inadvertently lose the "edge" from our ministry. Intercessors can pray and get no answers to their prayers; evangelists can preach their heart out and see no converts; teachers can preach and no one gets blessed; we can counsel for hours and see no problems resolved and no lives turned around.

In a powerful article on this theme, the late Christian teacher and author Arthur Wallis points out some of the places where we can lose ax-heads.

> Where you allowed bitterness and unforgiveness
> to seep into your relationship.
> Where your motives were corrupted by pride,
> greed or competitiveness.
> Where you got angry with God because of what
> He allowed or didn't allow.
> Where your dedication was defiled by a worldly
> spirit.[1]

We must do as this student did if we would recover that missing edge to our ministry.

1. Go and tell the Lord that you have lost it

Cry out. Do some shrieking, and get desperate. "Oh my Lord! It was borrowed!"

2. Answer honestly the question "Where did it fall?"

Have you gone too far sexually with your boyfriend? Have you shelved and neglected your Bible? Is there an unresolved argument still continuing between you and your wife? Are you critical and complaining about the leaders God has set over you?

3. Use the means of recovery

Elisha threw in a "dead stick." Prayer, repentance, renewed fellowship, or reading God's Word might all seem like a bunch of dead sticks to you now, but use them anyway and see what happens. God usually goes to work in new ways in our lives through old appointed means. Don't neglect them.

4. Let it first sink in the Jordan

The Jordan is a type of death in the Bible: it signifies separation. Sometimes we have to lose something before it can be found. The river of death swallows it up, and only God can bring about its recovery. Sometimes God calls us to loose our hold on our ministries—if they never return they were not really ours to use in the first place. If we get them back it is because God truly gave them to us.

5. When God gives it back, grasp it with enthusiasm

If God miraculously restores what you lost so carelessly, then take it back with both hands. Work even harder, be more adventurous, take some risks, use what you have, and allow nothing to go rusty through neglect or improper maintenance.

There it is. I've told you what really happened, and I hope that you believe it. God is working things out for your good. When others fall away or you face resistance, He wants you to grow and prosper. If you encounter "accidents" or setbacks in your service for Him, He still wants you to know that He is with you. If you become blunted or even lose your edge altogether, God can restore your spiritual effectiveness.

---

1. Arthur Wallis, "Lost your Cutting Edge?" *Restoration Magazine* (January/February 1988).

HELP—WE'RE SURROUNDED 12

2 Kings 6:8-23

Sometimes the church feels like an army in an old war film. In our own eyes we resemble nothing more than a platoon totally surrounded by the enemy, hopelessly outnumbered, with dwindling ammunition and little chance of rescue unless the heavenly cavalry turns up before we're all wiped out. Our next episode in Elisha's remarkable career has been penned in order to assure us that this scenario is not entirely accurate. Of course, some of the details may be true, but God wants us to see our own siege situations in an entirely different light. Like Elisha himself, if you and I are truly functioning as God's men and women where we are, then we are almost certainly either a potential or an actual threat to Satan's ploy and intentions in that location. As such you will be a marked man or woman, a target for his attack. In spite of this, however, the last state you should fall into is one of fear. Someone has calculated that there are no fewer than 366 direct instructions in the Bible not to fear—that's one for every day of the year including a leap year! It is not so much the fact that we are afraid which matters, it is what we do with our fears. What are we to do? The simplest answer to that is "Tread upon them!" Then we must carry on undeterred in the route God has marked out for us.

"There's a war on!"

> Now the king of Aram was at war with Israel.
> After conferring with his officers, he said, "I will
> set up my camp in such and such a place." The
> man of God sent word to the king of Israel:
> "Beware of passing that place, because the
> Arameans are going down there." So the king of
> Israel checked on the place indicated by the man
> of God. Time and again Elisha warned the king,
> so that he was on his guard in such places (2 Kings
> 6:8-10).

The prophet Elisha is a wonderful example of a man of God
who persevered in his responsibilities regardless of all threats and
intimidations which blockaded his way. The narrative opens with
the report of potentially life-threatening circumstances; circumstances in which we may find ourselves every day of our lives. We
live in a war zone. We did not start this war, for it commenced
millennia before we were born, but we have chosen on which side
we will fight.

For Elisha the problem was clear. The Aramean king, Ben-
Hadad (Naaman's monarch), had proved to be a constant irritant to
Israel. Frequent border raids were mounted on Jordan's territory in
Northern Israel. From 2 Kings 5:18 we know that Ben-Hadad
regularly worshiped at the temple of Rimmon, the Syrian god of
war. We come to resemble what we most worship: it wasn't possible for this ruler to glorify the god of war without becoming
aggressive, acquisitive, and war-like himself. Behind these border
raids, then, we can see the invisible intervention of a demonic
power throwing down a gauntlet to the God of Israel Himself. The
motive behind these acts of piracy and aggression was a diabolical
lust for power over the people of God themselves, and, therefore,
over the God of Israel. We can hear it in his reported words, "I will

set up camp. . . ." That's devil's talk.

This is the same war which continues to this day. It is a war for physical territory and for the spiritual allegiance of mankind. In nation after nation and state after state, the fight is on for the control and disciplining of the populations of those kingdoms. Like Elisha, God's people live in independence of the state but not in isolation from it. We are there to speak out during times of crisis, to warn of impending danger, and to point the way to the true source of deliverance and direction. We are to be the eyes and ears of men and women who are both blind and deaf to spiritual realities. More importantly, we are to be a voice for God in those situations.

The greatest safeguard for any nation is the presence of Christian people within it, but they have to be people of the right caliber—truly Spirit-filled, fearless, and prophetic. Elisha was given supernatural "intelligence" concerning enemy positions and enemy maneuvers. God sees men. He sees their movements, He even reads their minds. It is futile for either men or devils to think that they can outmaneuver the Lord. God knows and anticipates Satan's every move.

This explains why Elisha's prophetic information was so accurate. It was not vague and ambiguous, it was verifiable. Dates, places, times and even speed of movement were all precisely foretold and later proved to be accurate. This is the kind of prophetic edge we need as the people of God today. We need to know when, how, and where the next attacks will come, and it seems that God Himself is prepared to tell us not only this kind of information, but also what is to be done about it.

They're after you!

But be warned! If the people of God cultivate the ability to hear from God with this degree of accuracy then we will inevitably be targeted by special enemy death squads for assassination and removal from the scene of battle. You will be singled out for attack.

> This enraged the king of Aram. He summoned his officers and demanded of them, "Will you not tell me which of us is on the side of the king of Israel?" "None of us, my lord the king," said one of his officers, "but Elisha, the prophet who is in Israel, tells the king of Israel the very words you speak in your bedroom." "Go, find out where he is," the king ordered, "so I can send men and capture him." The report came back: "He is in Dothan." Then he sent horses and chariots and a strong force there. They went by night and surrounded the city. When the servant of the man of God got up and went out early the next morning, an army with horses and chariots had surrounded the city. "Oh, my lord, what shall we do?" the servant asked (2 Kings 6:11-15).

Elisha became the focus of the aggression and personal hostility of Ben-Hadad and presumably of the demonic entity, Rimmon, who pulled Ben-Hadad's strings. Initially, Ben-Hadad naturally assumed he had a fifth columnist, or spy, working in the Syrian camp—a double agent among his closest army officers who was acting as an informer for the enemy. A worldly man himself, he had no idea about the operations and gifts of the Holy Spirit and the way that they function among the people of God. He suspected that he had a traitor in the camp. He reminds us of those who turn up at church and hear the preacher, who happens to be a complete stranger to them, tell their life story. The reaction is invariably, "Who told him about me? Who passed on those details that he could speak so pointedly about me in that way?" And the answer, of course, is "God did!"

One of Ben-Hadad's officers knew this and told the hapless king the truth—even God's enemies acknowledge that the man of God is the best defense that Israel has. "Elisha the prophet . . . tells the king of Israel the very words you speak in your bedroom" (v 12). Yes, prophets know the secrets of men's hearts. When this happens, those unmasked in this way will either fall on their knees and lay down their sword saying, "God is really among you!" (1 Cor. 14:25), or they will climb on their horses, unsheathe their swords and say, "God help you!" Amazing, isn't it? The officers knew only what the king said in his briefing sessions, but Elisha knew what the king said in his bedroom. The officers knew only what the king chose to reveal, but God's prophets know what the king chooses not to reveal. This is why prophets became the focus of particular animosity and attack, and so, before long, Elisha's place of residence in Dothan was completely surrounded by Aramean cavalry, each man armed to the teeth, each one under strict orders to return with Elisha bound and gagged.

It is one thing to have a reputation among men for being spiritually effective; it is quite another thing to have that reputation in hell. You can tell the caliber of any man or woman by the kind of enemies that they make. If the Devil hates you and wicked men speak ill of you, then you must be in the same team as Elisha. Elisha earned the right reputation by being in the right place saying the right things to the right people on behalf of the right God. That's what put him at odds with Ben-Hadad, and that is why Ben-Hadad added the name of Elisha to his hit-list and dispatched the Syrian Central Intelligence Agency to establish the prophet's whereabouts. Ben-Hadad sent a very large force after Elisha; some might even call it "overkill." Does it suggest that the enemy is more scared of us than we are aware? I think so. This is not to minimize the danger in which we can often find ourselves, for it is very real. Some of Satan's hit squads may well have us on their secret agenda. What are we meant to do if Satan puts a contract out on our lives in this way?

We have two choices. We can react like Elisha did, or we can choose the response of his servant. The servant panicked, "Oh, my lord, what shall we do?" The longer you gaze on a difficulty the bigger it appears to be, unless God enables you to see through it. Many of God's people are so filled with fear that they spend the whole of their lives running from something that God will never allow to catch them. They fear cancers, car accidents, madness, poverty, and death. The Devil exploits all of these fears and more, fueling them with obsessive thoughts and even curses like "You will die young like your grandmother," "You are doomed to be a failure . . . your father was," "Go on that mission trip to India and the Devil will kill you," "That lump in your breast is almost certainly malignant." Fear is meditating upon the devil's lies. Faith is meditating on the promises and power of God. So often the greatness of our fears shows us the feebleness of our faith.

God is in charge

> "Don't be afraid," the prophet answered. "Those who are with us are more than those who are with them." And Elisha prayed, "O LORD, open his eyes so that he may see." Then the LORD opened the servant's eyes, and he looked and saw the hills full of horses and chariots of fire all around Elisha (2 Kings 6:16-17).

Being around Elisha must have been something like a regular visit to a spiritual beauty parlor—you always came away with a faith lift! It is so important that we hang around God's prophets during a time of trouble. Prophets represent a God Who is not afraid. Ever. And so Elisha speaks out and says two things to his servant. First, "Stop panicking!" and second, "Start trusting!"

1. Stop panicking

"Don't be afraid ... those who are with us are more than those who are with them." Fear opens the door to the very things of which we are afraid. The truth is, we fear men and devils so much because we fear God so little. Don't let the Devil intimidate you by threats and frightening appearances. It bothers me that so many Christians are so scared of demons. It is a fear, I am sure, that has been fueled by "portraits" and depictions of demons on rock album covers, video cases, horror movie posters, and even Christian novels. They are enough to give anyone nightmares! And yet we have to say quite candidly that most of this is bluff. Have you ever seen a cockroach, a spider, or even a bed-mite magnified under a microscope? Horrific, isn't it? But see these creatures shrink to their true proportions and while you still may not like them, you see how foolish those fears really are. Why, all you need to do is stamp on them! The Bible says, "The God of peace will soon crush Satan under your feet" (Rom. 16:20), and Jesus assured his disciples, "I have given you authority to trample on snakes and scorpions and to overcome all the power of the enemy; nothing will harm you" (Luke 10:19). That should shrink the enemy down to size a little, and shrink our fears also. The Devil may be powerful, but he is not all-powerful. He is a creature, and like all creatures he and his demons are subject to the Creator, so don't panic.

2. Start trusting

"Those who are with us are more than those who are with them." The Bible assures us repeatedly of the unseen forces, angelic hosts, and invisible powers which surround and protect the people of God. "The angel of the LORD encamps around those who fear him, and he delivers them" (Ps. 34:7). "If you make the Most High your dwelling—even the LORD, who is my refuge—then no harm will befall you, no disaster will come near your tent. For he will command his angels concerning you to guard you in all your ways" (Ps. 91:9-10). "The one who is in you is greater than the one who is in the world" (1 John 4:4). One interpretation of the "third of the stars in heaven" that fell with the Red Dragon, Satan, as recorded in Revelation 12, is that they represent one-third of the angelic hosts once loyal to God. If so, then that still leaves two-thirds submitted to Yahweh and fighting for Him on behalf of His people. Think of Jesus asleep in the back of a boat during the devil-whipped storm on Galilee as He and the disciples cross to Gadara to deal with the demoniac "Legion." When He is finally aroused, Jesus stands up and shouts, "Quiet! Be muzzled!" as if He's rebuking a barking dog, and the sea is instantly calm (Mark 4:35-41). In Christ, we have authority over demonic attacks upon ourselves or our loved ones.

O Lord, open his eyes

It is fascinating to note that while the rest of us have to take this by faith, Elisha requested that his servant be enabled to see, and with that, the servant saw into another world, the world that lies parallel to our own, the sphere inhabited by the invisible agents of God. The hills were full of the assembled armies of angelic beings in the appearance of horses and fiery chariots. The Bible assures us that these angels not only encamp around us as the people of God (Ps. 91:11-12), they also minister to the protection and other needs of God's heirs (Heb. 1:14). This fact is amply demonstrated both in Scripture and in church history. The imprisoned apostle Peter was twice miraculously released from his dungeon by angelic intervention (Acts 5:19; 12:6-10)—in the latter case it was to save him from imminent execution. Jesus assured the same Peter in Gethsemane that his misguided attempt to defend Jesus from arrest was superfluous, since He had at His command no fewer than 72,000 angels as His personal bodyguard, should they be required (Matt. 26:53). Though we have no warrant automatically to attribute intervention to angels, the fact remains that as a nation we in the U.K. have seen a remarkable turn of events many times in our history. In 1558, the Spanish Armada was devastated by freak storms. In 1940, 200,000 allied servicemen were successfully evacuated from the beaches of Dunkirk during four days of extraordinarily calm weather which many believe was a direct answer to the prayers of thousands.

When the vehicle of the church appears to skid, and the human agents responsible for its safety seem to lose control, it is good to know that God still has His hands very much upon the wheel. Individual believers should be like those old whistling kettles; when we are up to our necks in hot water and the heat is really on, then we should still find time to sing!

Take charge—God is in you

As the enemy came down toward him, Elisha prayed to the LORD, "Strike these people with blindness." So he struck them with blindness, as Elisha had asked.

Elisha told them, "This is not the road and this is not the city. Follow me, and I will lead you to the man you are looking for." And he led them to Samaria.

After they entered the city, Elisha said, "LORD, open the eyes of these men so they can see." Then the LORD opened their eyes and they looked, and there they were, inside Samaria.

When the king of Israel saw them, he asked Elisha, "Shall I kill them, my father? Shall I kill them?"

"Do not kill them," he answered. "Would you kill men you have captured with your own sword or bow? Set food and water before them so that they may eat and drink and then go back to their master." So he prepared a great feast for them, and

after they had finished eating and drinking, he
sent them away, and they returned to their master.
So the bands from Aram stopped raiding Israel's
territory (2 Kings 6:18-23).

Elisha now moves on to the offensive, primarily engaging the
weapon of prayer. Even in this, Elisha is a model of God's merciful treatment of his enemies. Elisha did not pray for their
destruction, but only for further deception. He asked God to close
the Arameans' eyes in a manner exactly the opposite to the opening of those of his servant. Their senses were dulled and four results
followed: they couldn't read faces so they didn't recognize Elisha;
they couldn't read maps, so they didn't know where they were; they
couldn't follow road signs, so they didn't recognize the route into
the city; and they couldn't see any danger so they didn't know that
Elisha led them into Israel's equivalent of Aldershot army camp—
right into Joram's barracks and the clutches of the Israelite army.
The same God who bound the enemy in answer to prayer now
loosed them to see their perilous condition (v 20). Blind eyes now
opened and in a flash they saw faces, read the map, saw the road
signs, and recognized their danger. Their ambush had gone horri-
bly wrong.

Understandably, King Joram wanted to seize the opportunity
to butcher the elite of Aram's military forces. This is the spirit of
revenge manifesting itself with a vengeance. I recall reading how
Abe Lemmons was once sacked from his position as coach of the
Longhorns basketball team in Texas. When asked if he was bitter
toward De Loss, the manager who fired him, Lemmons replied,
"Not at all, but I do plan to buy a glass-bottomed car so I can see
the look on his face when I run over him." Revenge we can understand, but Elisha's response requires some explanation, for Elisha
said, "Do not kill them."

As far as Elisha was concerned it was the Lord who captured
the Arameans, and it was the Lord's prerogative alone to decide

their fate. What God directed that day exceeded everyone's expectations. God told Elisha to arrange a banquet of roast meat and the best vintage wine from Joram's wine cellars. The Arameans were not to be harmed in any way. They were not paraded in chains on public television looking frightened and defeated, nor were they imprisoned in Israeli military installations to act as a human shield in case of further Aramean incursions on Hebrew land. They weren't even thrown into crowded internment camps for the duration of the war. Instead they were treated with a totally unpredictable kindness and then redirected safely back to Aramean headquarters.

"If your enemy is hungry, feed him; if he is thirsty, give him something to drink. In doing this, you will heap burning coals on his head" (Rom. 12:20). This is how we are to overcome evil with good (Rom. 12:21). The demons which had operated in and through the Aramean troops were now bound and defeated. In the same way the people who oppose the church and her Lord today are the dupes of the Devil. Our real enemies are not people. We can afford both to speak and act kindly toward those who try to harm us—just as Elisha gave the Aramean soldiers food, drink, their Red Cross parcels, permission to write a postcard home, new maps and compasses, and clear directions back to the comfort of home, so we can afford to be generous with our enemies. Love your enemies— it will drive them nuts! Since we cannot get back at our enemies any other way, it's as well we realize that nothing unsettles an enemy quite so much as forgiving him. Elisha killed Israel's enemies with kindness and for the time being at least all Aramean raids stopped.

When you're tempted to run from the battle

The story of the siege of Dothan stands in Scripture as a vivid reminder that our safety and security lie in the Lord and not in the power of mere men. Grateful as we are for stable government and the protective agencies of police, army, navy, or air force, we know that none of these can effectively protect any of us against a really determined assassin—and Satan is a really determined assassin! But Jesus said, "I hold the keys of Death and Hades" (Rev. 1:18), and those keys no longer swing on Satan's belt. Our enemies are now God's enemies and the Lord has sworn to protect us. When we hear the words "Your days are numbered," since they come from the Lord's lips they no longer serve as a threat but as a promise. We are truly immortal until our life's work is done.

The enemy is always outnumbered because one man or woman with God is in the majority. You are therefore safe to get on with your life's work. Like Elisha our task is fourfold; we are to warn the unwary by our prophetic words, encourage the fearful by our prophetic vision, confound the enemy by our prophetic prayer, and deliver the condemned by our show of prophetic mercy. We have too much to be getting on with to be worried about saving our own skin—better leave that to God. He's rather good at it.

WHO HAS BELIEVED THE REPORT OF THE LORD?

2 Kings 6:24-7:20

13

Aggression stimulates defense and the preoccupation with defense against a backdrop of aggression usually leads to a siege mentality. History is patterned with episodes of man's aggression against his fellow men. There are raiders who plunder the stored wealth of others on a seasonal basis simply because those raiders live a parasitic lifestyle maintained by the fat, flesh, and life-blood of others. There are violent, mindless acts of vandalism, motiveless attacks upon the life and property of others governed by the sheer hellish excitement that comes when might asserts itself over weakness and raw power feeds on the thrill of rape, murder, pillage, and destruction.

Nevertheless, history is also punctuated with the remarkable stories of the heroism of besieged communities summoned to acts of incredible bravery against incalculable odds. So inspiring are these stories that in the twentieth century stirring films have been made of some of the most famous—Leonidas and his three hundred Spartans defending the pass of Thermopylae against the Persians; the Athenian stand against 50,000 of those Persians some ten years earlier on the plain of Marathon; General Gordon's resistance to the death against the invading Muslim Dervishes at Khartoum in the Sudan; Davy Crockett with his 130 Texans at the siege of the Alamo holding out against the 4,000 Mexican troops of Santa Ana—these are just a few examples of these heroic stands.

As far as I know, no one has ever filmed the even more spectacular deliverance from almost certain death which unfolded in the incident which will occupy our attention as we turn to the next astonishing chapter in Elisha's career—the siege of Samaria.

The story opens with another of the now familiar glimpses of a culture in trouble and a church in deadly crisis. It is the story of a city under siege by dark forces which have mobilized a frighteningly well-equipped army as their agents to terrorize and intimidate the backslidden people of God.

> Some time later, Ben-Hadad king of Aram mobilized his entire army and marched up and laid siege to Samaria (2 Kings 6:24).

I have never lived through a siege, but it takes little imagination for us to know that it must be a very frightening experience. The sense of confinement must be very disturbing, the feeling that there is no escape because the enemy surrounds the defended area and flight is impossible. The defending walls must seem very much lower and very much thinner than they appeared to be during less dangerous times; at any point the enemy could breach or scale those flimsy battlements. Smug boasting and contented laughter about the bravery of the defenders, the superiority of their weapons and the volume of their stored supplies, which at one time convinced the beleaguered that they could hold out forever, must rapidly give way to sober realism and an honest appraisal that the picture is not as bright as it once appeared to be. In their fear, a warm camaraderie must give way to a lonely dog-eat-dog fight for personal survival as the situation becomes more critical. Death itself, which once looked such a remote possibility, is probably never far from the anxious thoughts of even the most ardent freedom fighter confined within limits of the besieged fortress. It takes little thought and even less imagination to see that we too are surrounded, in moral and spiritual decline and in desperate need of a divine intervention.

Seeing the world as God sees it

The story now penetrates the thick walls of the Samaritan defenses and gives us a glimpse into the desperate state of the community life of the frightened people "holed up" in the city. It is not a pretty picture. It is marked by several ugly characteristics.

1. Famine

> There was a great famine in the city; the siege lasted so long that a donkey's head sold for eighty shekels of silver, and a quarter of a cab of seed pods for five shekels (2 Kings 6:25).

This is, of course, a typical consequence of military conflict and a protracted siege. Food becomes scarce even on the black market, and as the quality of what is available declines, the prices paid for it rapidly climb to unbelievable heights. It must have been a long time since donkey's head featured on Israeli menus, and don't be fooled by the NIV's euphemistic "seed pods": in reality this was "dove's dung"—a week's wage for the refuse of the bottom of a bird cage, and two months" salary for the least edible part of a donkey (if donkeys are edible at all!). I once heard Canadian Bible teacher Ern Baxter refer to a donkey's head as the best symbol of what unaided human wisdom can produce, and dove's dung as what's left in the church when the Holy Ghost has departed.

In the eighth century B.C. the prophet Amos predicted

> "The days are coming," declares the Sovereign LORD, "when I will send a famine throughout the

land—not a famine of food or a thirst for water,
but a famine of hearing the words of the LORD.
Men will stagger from sea to sea and wander from
north to east, searching for the word of the LORD,
but they will not find it" (Amos 8:11-12).

We live in a time of famine like this today. Listen to the content-
less drivel uttered by supposedly intelligent politicians and sample the
refuse, offal, and dung presented as spiritual nourishment by many of
the church's officially ordained ministers and you'll understand something of the seriousness of our crisis. And of course, none of this
"wisdom" comes cheaply. Millions of dollars are wasted upon useless
bureaucracy and empty religious activity; armies of civil servants run
around, feverishly presenting solutions to our ills, while parades of
religious cults and silver-tongued spiritual leaders announce confi-
dently their new doctrines for a new age. They cost much and don't
satisfy. Drippy, driveling speeches and sermonettes with no edge, no
power, no truth, and no unction are the verbal diet of the hungry
masses under spiritual siege in our nation. The king complained that
there was nothing on the threshing floor and nothing in the winepress (v 27); spiritually speaking his people were without even the
necessities for living, and this is also our condition today.

2. Devaluation of human life

As the king of Israel was passing by on the wall, a
woman cried to him, "Help me, my lord the king!"
The king replied, "If the LORD does not help you,
where can I get help for you? From the threshing
floor? From the winepress?" Then he asked her,
"What's the matter?"
She answered, "This woman said to me, 'Give
up your son so that we may eat him today, and
tomorrow we'll eat my son.' So we cooked my son

and ate him. The next day I said to her, 'Give up your son so that we may eat him,' but she had hidden him"(2 Kings 6:26-29).

The weak were the first to suffer. It was considered an economic necessity of the times to allow the vulnerable in Samaritan society to forfeit their lives in order to sustain the existence of the rest, and so they resorted to infanticide and to cannibalism. The natural affection a mother should have for her own offspring was stifled and suppressed, and even little children were killed, cooked and then eaten so that they would not only cease to be a burden upon society but also benefit others by their deaths.

Our initial shock and recoil at such horrors yields to deeper disgust at the realization that such obscenities are being daily repeated in our own day. Abortion, infanticide, and euthanasia are now considered either legal or at least morally acceptable practices in Western society. The rationale behind each of these acts is partly economic, dictated by the "strains" the sustenance of unwanted human life would place upon both private and government funding. Uglier still is the sordid gain and profiteering of the agencies which traffic in this trade. The "abortuaries" make millions each year, and the increasing trade in fetal organs and body parts begins to resemble more and more the Nazi trade in similar macabre "goods" from the Jewish victims of the Holocaust. For example, the Diabetes Treatment Project at UCLA is using pancreases from late-term aborted infants in its experimental projects. Rabies vaccine has also been developed from viruses grown in the lungs of aborted fetuses. Even more incredible is the fact that a cosmetics firm in France has developed a facial cream designed to "rejuvenate the skin" manufactured partly from cells derived from the tissue of aborted babies. In parts of America developing embryos and body parts from "the products of an abortion" are being encased in transparent plastic and sold as novelties and "good luck" charms in fancy goods boutiques.

Cannibalism is the consumption of the flesh of other human beings for power and personal profit. What are the examples listed above if they are not another form of cannibalism, a cannibalism made all the more reprehensible because it occurs not in pagan, primitive societies, but in modern, sophisticated Western communities?

3. Impotent, faithless leadership

> When the king heard the woman's words, he tore his robes. As he went along the wall, the people looked, and there, underneath, he had sackcloth on his body. He said, "May God deal with me, be it ever so severely, if the head of Elisha son of Shaphat remains on his shoulders today!" (2 Kings 6:30-31).

The king mounted a show of piety at this difficult time for his people, but it was merely a front for deep irreverence. He wore sackcloth (a sign of sorrow and penitence) in order to signal to God his concern for the people, but this was worn under his usual garments in a hidden way. It was merely token piety, indulged as a form of "hedging one's bets" and not the sincere expression of total dependence upon God. The king was too dignified truly to repent, and behind the mask of religious posturing beat a heart at war with God. He had already blamed God for the city's plight in verse 27, and now he came to vent that anger by vowing to destroy God's prophet, Elisha.

Here, then, is an example of weak leadership which had the ability to see nothing but the immediate problem and the immediate need. Behind all blame shifting, and particularly the ugly way in which we sometimes off-load blame on to God, is a refusal or inability to trace the moral and spiritual problems which are the real cause of our difficulties. The king was to rend his garments, but he refused to rend his heart. He was a man at odds with his Creator and argumentative with God's Word. Stupid leadership is like this. Prophets are sent by God to enable us to read reality correctly, to give us an alternative perspective which is more penetrating than the current wisdom, but the royal reading of reality was impatient with the divine perspective. It plotted to decapitate God's servant in an attempt to silence God's Word.

Yet, as we have seen, God's servants are immortal until their life's work is done, and it is invigorating to see the scene change to the dwelling of Elisha where the suppressed despair of the siege with its attendant fear and hopelessness has gained no foothold whatsoever.

The saving presence of the people of God

The greatest hope for the frightened nations of our frightening world is the presence of vibrant, faith-filled believers in their midst. Elisha again plays a key role in bringing about reversal and change. During times of crisis many men and women are merely an *echo* of the consensus opinion of the crowd, when what we most need to hear is a *voice* which speaks with the originality and freshness that come from contact with the living God. Elisha shows us three dimensions of that voice.

1. The voice of rebuke

> Now Elisha was sitting in his house, and the elders were sitting with him. The king sent a messenger ahead, but before he arrived, Elisha said to the elders, "Don't you see how this murderer is sending someone to cut off my head? Look, when the messenger comes, shut the door and hold it shut against him. Is not the sound of his master's footsteps behind him?" (2 Kings 6:32).

The city elders of Samaria may well have shared the king's contempt for Elisha during times of prosperity, but they knew where to be during a time of crisis. They came to the home of God's man convinced that here was one place where they would be spared from hearing the clichés of high-sounding political rhetoric or the pious gush of religious twaddle. Prophets see what others don't see, hear what others can't hear, and say what others daren't say. Elisha unmasked the reality of the situation. He called King Joram a murderer, a fact which those elders should have seen, addressed, and resolved. Sadly, they were cowards, one of the least desirable qualities to be expected within leaders. So often a people get the government and leadership they deserve—pity the people whose leaders are wimps. Wimps turn a blind eye and keep their mouths shut about evil. They love their own skins more than they love to see truth and right prevail. This is why it is so refreshing to hear Elisha's outspoken denunciation of the king's true intents. We need more men and women of this breed.

2. The voice of hope

> Elisha said, "Hear the word of the LORD. This is what the LORD says: About this time tomorrow, a seah of flour will sell for a shekel and two seahs of barley for a shekel at the gate of Samaria" (2 Kings 7:1).

As God's ambassador, Elisha is privy to secret information which has hitherto been concealed from the general populace. Elisha was the representative of a gracious and merciful God Who does not treat us as our sins deserve, and Who can totally reverse our bad fortune, often for no other reason than the pleasure He takes in being gracious to the undeserving. Elisha announced the imminent end of famine conditions. He told the elders and their murderous king that in spite of their cynicism and impertinent unbelief God would bring about such abundance of supply within the space of twenty-four hours that prices would drop through the floor for those same staple foods which hitherto had been unobtainable.

Today God's prophets are lifting the church's eyes once more, to see the glorious prospects God holds out for His people. He wants to use a transformed church to transform the world. The spiritual famine can and will end, because God is about to send us abundant supplies of His word and His Spirit, of truth and power, in order that our renewed proclamation of good news may be matched by authoritative confirmation of good deeds. We are about to see a global recovery of the apostolic gospel of the kingdom, together with the apostolic anointing of signs and wonders which ought to accompany it (Mark 16:15-20; Acts 4:29-31; Rom. 15:18-20; 1 Thes. 1:4-5). This global advance may have been hindered in previous generations, but it cannot be halted in the generations yet to come. The greatest chapters of church history are yet to be written.

3. The voice of judgment

> The officer on whose arm the king was leaning said to the man of God, "Look, even if the LORD should open the floodgates of the heavens, could this happen?" (2 Kings 7:2).

Unbelief is so arrogant! It dares to voice its dim and misguided perceptions in the very face of the Lord's emphatic declarations. The stupid officer who blurted out his doubts so freely represents all those in the world or the church who question the power or willingness of God to bring sudden deliverance to His people. This is the "natural mind" of man doing its stuff, doing what comes naturally to it—arguing with the Word of God. It is this mind which not only cannot receive the things of God, it deems them "foolish" (1 Cor. 2:14).

Unbelief explicitly questions what God has said and vaunts human reason over divine revelation. It attempts to set limits to the power of God and in some cases succeeds. "Jesus could do no mighty works there because of their unbelief" (Mark 6:5-6), would be an accurate summary of many towns and churches in England and America today. But such unbelief is culpable and stands under God's judgment. One form that judgment may take is for the Lord to ratify it by leaving it to the results of its own hardness and misalignment with reality. This was the judgment pronounced by Elisha upon the skeptical commanding officer: *"You will see it with your own eyes, but you will not eat any of it!"*

Don't talk yourself or your church out of blessing. If in doubt, keep your mouth shut. Watch your language or you may curse your life with the fulfillment of your weary expectations and your dull, dead hope. On the other hand, this is the time for God's prophets to speak out as Elisha did, to refuse to be an echo and prove rather to be a voice which will expose sin, expound its remedy and expel unbelief.

The agents of change

When God begins to signal change on a large scale for a beleaguered people, He often begins in surprising quarters. Present conditions set no limits to what God can do, and a miraculous intervention of God was already under way even as Elisha spoke, just as it is in the world today. The Lord Jesus is breathing fresh life and fresh hope into His church, and a "new thing" is happening among His people, in every denomination and upon every continent. This wave of the Holy Spirit's activity will touch people at the personal, corporate, and even national level. It will engage vast numbers in individual, ecclesiastical, and universal renewal. The implications are cosmic.

The despised

Meanwhile, of course, it does not appear that these effects are even remotely possible. For one thing, God has begun with those despised by society.

> Now there were four men with leprosy at the
> entrance of the city gate. They said to each other,
> "Why stay here until we die?" (2 Kings 7:3).

God uses the disreputable. These lepers bore the stigma of an incurable skin disease and were therefore ostracized, outcasts of society, excluded from the mainstream of the city's life, psychologically defeated and withdrawn—a bit like some Christians, in fact. God doesn't usually begin His recovery and revival program in the church's major seminaries, denominational headquarters, or among its high-flying intellectuals and leading agencies. He uses unknowns, outcasts, and objects of derision—people like you and me. You may well live to make discoveries and voice announcements which could change the world!

The desperate
These people were also desperate for change.

> Now there were four men with leprosy at the
> entrance of the city gate. They said to each other,
> "Why stay here until we die? If we say, 'We'll go
> into the city'—the famine is there, and we will die.
> And if we stay here, we will die. So let's go over to
> the camp of the Arameans and surrender. If they
> spare us, we live; if they kill us, then we die" (2
> Kings 7:3-4).

People who talk like this have shaken off the casual apathy and resignation to death which marks their contemporaries. Desperate times call for desperate people and this kind of desperation refuses to accept the status quo. Instead, it climbs out of the rut and resolves to look for solutions or to die in the attempt.

The daring

Furthermore, they were daring in action—and so prepared to risk all.

> "If they spare us, we live; if they kill us, then we die." At dusk they got up and went to the camp of the Arameans (2 Kings 7:4-5).

They had lost their smugness about starving to death and were prepared to take a risk. A "do-nothing" fatalism has to yield to a "risk-all" faith. There was a reckless pioneer spirit about these lepers which refused to die amid Samaria's ancient traditions. Like Esther, they said, "If I perish, I perish" (Es. 4:16) concluding, quite rightly, that they had nothing to lose and quite possibly everything to gain.

In every awakening or new move of the Holy Spirit, God has an advance guard who venture to make new discoveries of His grace and goodness, people who are prepared to step out of the norm and to walk into new experiences. They usually carry a measure of stigma and ostracism for doing so, yet the price is considered small change when compared to the blessing they hold in prospect. This was the experience of the prominent leaders during the Great Awakening in the 1740s when men like George Whitefield and John and Charles Wesley sought God in their desperation for personal and national revival. It was true also for the early pioneers of the Pentecostal movement around 1907, both in America and in Europe, and the same features marked the beginnings of the worldwide charismatic movement from the 1960s onward, when many pastors and leaders in the mainstream denominations paid a price for embracing so enthusiastically this new move of the Holy Spirit. Some were regarded as heretics and others as insane. Some forfeited their prestigious posts and were fired from their positions or ostracized by their denominations.

In this connection it is worth noting that these four lepers made their discovery with their feet, not their heads. They did not understand fully nor see clearly what lay ahead of them. Some things you have to believe before you can see, and God honors our willingness to make the venture. Jesus said once to a religious but highly skeptical audience who were resistant to His claims, "If anyone chooses to do God's will, he will find out whether my teaching comes from God or whether I speak on my own" (John 7:17). Commitment invariably precedes full enlightenment, faith seeks understanding, risky actions make us eligible for rational explanations.

God has been at work, supernaturally panicking the Arameans by causing them to experience an auditory "hallucination," the menacing sound of an army, which they wrongly interpreted as an advancing force of Hittite and Egyptian mercenaries (vv 6-7). The Bible says, "The wicked man flees though no one pursues, but the righteous are as bold as a lion" (Prov. 28:1). The same Spirit Who emboldens believers to take courageous action when the odds are decidedly against their success can exploit the secret fears of unbelievers and cause them to flee when in fact they are in no real danger. The Arameans hastily fled in the early evening gloom and abandoned virtually everything they owned on the plains around Samaria, leaving behind a vast treasury just waiting to be plundered. The degree of fear which they felt is witnessed by the fact that they left their horses and donkeys—animals which would actually have hastened their flight had they been in a frame of mind to realize this. This must have been a very eerie sight for the lepers, but it was encountered by active faith and not theological inquiry—they walked out by faith; understanding was to come later.

The debtors

One last feature worth noting about these lepers is that they were debtors to others.

> The men who had leprosy reached the edge of the
> camp and entered one of the tents. They ate and

drank, and carried away silver, gold and clothes, and went off and hid them. They returned and entered another tent and took some things from it and hid them also.

Then they said to each other, "We're not doing right. This is a day of good news and we are keeping it to ourselves. If we wait until daylight, punishment will overtake us. Let's go at once and report this to the royal palace."

So they went and called out to the city gate-keepers and told them, "We went into the Aramean camp and not a man was there—not a sound of anyone—only tethered horses and donkeys, and the tents left just as they were."

The gatekeepers shouted the news, and it was reported within the palace (2 Kings 7:8-11).

It's amusing to see their quite natural reaction to their amazing discovery of the Aramean plunder. Like kids at Christmas they grabbed for each new package in sight, ripping the wrappings and clutching each amazing new find selfishly to their chests. It was a veritable Aladdin's cave of "goodies" just for them, and they behaved like selfish children.

No, more like selfish Christians if the exact parallel is to be drawn. So many turn fresh discoveries of the Lord's power into selfish pleasure trips of spiritual indulgence. We have our holy huddles and our bless-me clubs which lock God's blessings into our own private healing conferences, renewal retreats, doctrine clubs, and exclusive fellowship suppers while the world goes to hell. We loot God's blessings for ourselves alone. Like the lepers we must awaken to our obligations and our indebtedness to the "starving" multitudes around us. It is tragically possible to be utterly indifferent toward the moral, spiritual, and physical needs of our fellow men. Three convictions need to grip renewed, restored

Spirit-filled believers today.

1. It is not right to keep a good thing to yourself—it needs demonstration.
2. It is not right to keep good news to yourself—it needs proclamation.
3. It is not right to delay initiative indefinitely—it needs urgent action.

Someone has defined evangelism as "one satisfied beggar telling other hungry beggars where to find bread." That's what the lepers decided to do, and that's what we must do also. Our enormous spiritual privileges lay upon us a great spiritual responsibility. We are so hesitant to take action, so fearful of reaction, so afraid that our reports will be met with hostility or derision. The lepers were responsible only to report what they had found. What their hearers did with that news was not their problem. The primary reason I am and remain a Christian is because the Christian message is true. It is true and it works. Because it is true, I am obliged to proclaim it, to argue for its validity, to marshall its proofs, and to demonstrate its validity by "signs following." After that I can do no more. It is the facts which count, and the facts have to be told. This is the thrust of our indebtedness to others. We must both tell and show the truth of our message.

The lepers became witnesses. Witnesses report accurately what they have seen and heard—the verdict of the jury is not their responsibility. These "witnesses" told a very simple sequence of facts: that bread was available and where to get it. Furthermore, they were excited and no longer looked hungry. They witnessed by lip and by life. Which is the most important in our witness, what we say or how we live? Which is the most important wing on a passenger aircraft, the left one or the right one? They are both essential.

The varied reception to the changes God brings

We have been under siege. Massive forces of wickedness surround us and we appear to be hopelessly outnumbered, in danger of overwhelming assault and crushing defeat at the hands of the forces which oppose us. Yet as we have seen, God is encouraging us to see the possibility of a sudden divine intervention and reversal of our fortunes. Some have already begun to experience something of the possibilities which lie at hand. Like the four lepers, many of God's people have seen first hand what God can do with our enemies, putting them to panicked flight, freeing us to plunder their resources and to pass on the good news that we are saved—saved in every dimension. This is good news. It has to be passed on first to the church, and then to the world.

The sequel to the discovery is recorded in verses 11-20. It shows very clearly that responses to this news of renewal, restoration, and revival will be varied. Not everyone will receive what we have to report: some will not be pleased with what God is doing, and some will refuse to benefit from it.

> The gatekeepers shouted the news, and it was reported within the palace.
>
> The king got up in the night and said to his officers, "I will tell you what the Arameans have done to us. They know we are starving; so they have left the camp to hide in the countryside, thinking, 'They will surely come out, and then we will take them alive and get into the city.'"
>
> One of his officers answered, "Have some men take five of the horses that are left in the city. Their plight will be like that of all the Israelites left here—yes, they will only be like all these Israelites who are doomed. So let us send them to find out what happened."

So they selected two chariots with their horses, and the king sent them after the Aramean army. He commanded the drivers, "Go and find out what has happened."

They followed them as far as the Jordan, and they found the whole road strewn with the clothing and equipment the Arameans had thrown away in their headlong flight. So the messengers returned and reported to the king. Then the people went out and plundered the camp of the Arameans. So a seah of flour sold for a shekel, and two seahs of barley sold for a shekel, as the LORD had said (2 Kings 7:11-16).

A spectrum of reactions is recorded here.

Some are like the gatekeepers, the excitable type (v 11). They receive the message at once, even accompanied with appropriate emotions of joy and noisy excitement. In faith they believed "the report of the Lord" and what they believed in their hearts they confessed with their lips. Good news is worth shouting about.

Then there was the king, the skeptical type (v 12). The king placed the worst possible construction upon the facts reported by the lepers. He suspected a trick. He could see only a clever ruse designed by the Arameans to trap Israel and bring about her downfall. Like so many today, who see each new move of the Holy Spirit as a deception of the devil, the king suspected that only harm could come by following wild reports of blessing, and so he was fearful to the point of inaction and immobility.

Third, we see the reaction of the officer, the experimental type (vv 13-16). He was cautious, with numerous reservations about the validity of the good news he had heard, yet he was willing to check it out at first hand. He sent five of his men, men doomed to die anyway, in order to see if there was substance to the lepers" story. It's all right to reserve judgment so long as you will at least talk, read the literature, come to the meetings and see for yourself if the reports of God's power are true. You will find, as these soldiers did, that the famine is over and it is now possible to come and eat your fill.

The present renewal of the Holy Spirit has met with all these reactions. We expect skepticism from worldly people, but it is utterly misplaced in the church. Christians who profess to believe the Bible see there an open universe in which God intervenes frequently to save, deliver, heal, and restore. Yet these same believers meet current reports of advance, enlargement, visitation, and blessing with a cynical fear and unhealthy skepticism. Far better to check out these reports firsthand and test their validity both by their roots in God's Word and their fruits in people's lives. Why not enthusiastically welcome all that the Lord provides to satisfy your hunger and to deliver you from the shame of your defeat?

The officer who met Elisha's prophecy with such arrogant doubt and unbelief now experienced the downside of the people's eagerness to experience the fulfillment of God's word (vv 17-20). He was trampled and killed in the rush. Today, as in this remarkable incident, plenty of God's hungry people are rushing to experience God's miraculous provision for His beleaguered church. Stay cynically opposed to this and you will either starve or be killed in the rush. Since the global revival is coming, it is far better to be carried along in the flow of God's gracious purposes than to fall beneath it.

As for those of us who have begun to plunder the provision which we are convinced God has made for His people, let's take our cue from the four lepers. Let's stop our introverted patterns of self-indulgence and say with them, "We're not doing right. This is a day of good news and we are keeping it to ourselves.... Let's go at once and report this!"

Who knows? Somebody may believe us.

IS THERE A PROPHET IN THE HOUSE?

14

2 Kings 8:1-9:13

One of the greatest needs of the hour is the recovery of the prophet's ministry within the church. And yet, as is so often the case, what we most need is frequently what we least want. This is particularly true when we think of the prophetic word. To embrace prophetic ministry can be a bit like clutching a nettle or holding a poisonous asp to your chest—you are likely to get stung! And yet the venom which God's prophets carry is healing venom. If you can stand to be pierced by their words then you are likely to be healed; healed of the poisons, distortions, and unwelcome growths which threaten the spiritual health of Christ's body, the church.

God's "now" word

Prophecy is God's "now" word. It is a particular word for a particular people living at a particular time and in a particular place. Whenever it is given voice, it is revelatory of God's heart for us here and now. For the disobedient it announces warning of judgment and discloses God's hostility towards particular sins which debilitate the Christian community. For the obedient it takes the form of promise and signals God's intent to work restoration and recovery in the lives of those people. It is not equivalent to preaching though it may well be markedly present within the best preaching you have heard.

The term "prophecy" derives from two Greek words; *pro*—"for, on behalf of," and *phemi*—"to speak." It is to speak for or on behalf of another. In this case, the speaker acts as spokesperson to God. God is not a silent but a speaking God; a God who regularly complements the written, final, and complete testimony of Scripture with fresh bulletins to His people today.

In any discussion of the place and importance of the gift of prophecy today, it is important that we avoid two extremes. The first is the position of those who deny the validity of prophecy at all. Arguing rightly for a closed canon of Scripture they allow no room for God to speak to His people by any other means than the written word of Scripture. This is an untenable position, for apart from the fact that experience indicates that God does speak in extrabiblical ways, the Scriptures themselves encourage us to desire to prophesy (1 Cor. 14:1) and give us many criteria by which we can test such utterances as to their validity (1 Cor. 14:3; Matt. 7:15-20; 1 Thes. 5:19-21). The other extreme occurs within some charismatic groups where for all practical purposes prophecy is elevated to a position superior to Scripture. This can be seen by the gullible acceptance of "prophecies" without testing, no matter how bizarre they appear to be, and the way their expression crowds out the serious reading and exposition of Scripture in their regular meetings together.

We need to hear authentic prophecy. This is the way God wants His spokesmen and women to function—shattering the smothering layers of encrusted tradition which harden and immobilize the people of God, and quite literally freeing us to be ourselves, to become the men and women God made us to be by the renewing activity of the Holy Spirit within our hearts and lives. Prophetic preachers come to do for us what the Bible itself has been vested with power to do, namely, to create and to critique a new people.

Prophets must therefore be marked by great boldness of speech. In the New Testament "boldness" is the distinguishing mark of men and women who have been filled with the Spirit of God (Acts 4:29-31). The Greek term for this, *parrhesia*, literally means "all—speech" and describes the freedom which the Spirit gives individuals to enable them to say anything God gives without yielding to the temptation to withhold or to suppress the Spirit's prompting. It equates with our word "frankness" and means daring and accurate speech which bluntly and forthrightly tells it as it is; tells it in fact as God sees it, which is how it really is.

It is also undeniable that while prophets do not coerce or manipulate their vision into reality, nevertheless, because they speak God's words, then those words have an inherent creative power on account of God's anointing upon them, to bring into being the things of which they speak, to create the very realities they so beautifully describe. This is precisely why we need more prophets and prophecy today. Years ago the same opinion was expressed by the late A. W. Tozer whom many consider to have been a prophet himself: "We need to have the gifts of the Spirit restored again to the church, and it is my belief that the one gift we need most now is the gift of prophecy."

Prophets show us both what is descending from above and what is coming from the future. As Philip Greenslade writes, "The prophet brings the future into today and exhorts the church to live in the light of it. He brings true hope by eliminating wishful thinking. He is the enemy of fatalism and the friend of faith. He opposes panic but resists passivity just as strongly."[1]

Men and women of a prophetic bent of mind can be anointed by the Spirit actually to reshape the communities in which they are called to minister, and indeed, even to re-create the world in which they live. "Christian speakers do not merely massage the world as we find it. We create a new world."[2]

There is a new world coming, and that is why we are called not merely to cope with the world as it presently is but to change it.

The primary weapon we have to initiate and to maintain such God-ordained change, is truth spoken in the power of God's prophetic anointing. Truth however is a double-edged sword.

Elisha, the world-changer

The next chapters before us, 2 Kings 8-10, contain the narrative of Elisha's role in bringing about God's judicial sentence upon the royal house of Omri and the destruction of the last vestiges of Baalism in the northern kingdom. This is a goal partly realized by the anointing of a usurper, Jehu, who becomes the almost too-eager executioner, in God's hands, of the remaining members of that particular royal family. Elisha's prophetic words created these destructive changes. They also worked constructively to bring hope and restitution to a woman of good heart. In other words, when truth is spoken prophetically it becomes the means of both restoration and retribution: restoration is the experience of the righteous, and retribution is the experience of the wicked. Truth cuts both ways, and God's prophets are not afraid to speak with such a double-edged sword in their mouths (cf Rev. 1:16; 2:12; 19:15).

Three incidents demonstrate these aspects of the prophetic ministry.

Lighting the route-markers of divine restoration

> Now Elisha had said to the woman whose son he had restored to life, "Go away with your family and stay for a while wherever you can, because the LORD has decreed a famine in the land that will last for seven years." The woman proceeded to do as the man of God said. She and her family went away and stayed in the land of the Philistines for seven years.

At the end of the seven years she came back from the land of the Philistines and went to the king to beg for her house and land. The king was talking to Gehazi, the servant of the man of God, and had said, "Tell me about all the great things Elisha has done." Just as Gehazi was telling the king how Elisha had restored the dead to life, the woman whose son Elisha had brought back to life came to beg the king for her house and land.

Gehazi said, "This is the woman, my lord the king, and this is her son whom Elisha restored to life." The king asked the woman about it, and she told him.

Then he assigned an official to her case and said to him, "Give back everything that belonged to her, including all the income from her land from the day she left the country until now" (2 Kings 8:1-6).

Prophecy is God's "now" word. When authentic prophecy comes it has three major components which both the bearer and the recipient need to deal with. Ideally, we need to be accurate in all three, but very frequently while one part may be accurate, it is possible to be in error in the remaining two. The three ingredients are first revelation—the disclosure of hitherto secret or inaccessible information. God impresses upon the prophet in words or a picture (or sometimes a combination of both) the significant burden to be conveyed to the people.

Secondly, there is interpretation. Since many pictures are cryptic and do not yield their meaning very readily, it is important that we wait on God for the appropriate interpretation of the word or image which God has given.

Thirdly, there is application. We need to discover what it is that the Lord wants us to do about what we have heard or seen.

The practical implications of a picture are not always obvious. For example, in Acts 21:10-11 the prophet Agabus shared a picture with Paul and his companions. The picture involved Paul being symbolically tied up as a prediction that the apostle would soon be bound and handed over to the Romans when he reached Jerusalem. Paul's friends interpreted this as a warning that Paul should not proceed further, whereas Paul was undeterred in his intention to visit Jerusalem, and saw the prediction merely as an additional confirmation that he would suffer much at the hands of the Jews in their capital. Who was right? Should Paul have obeyed the advice of godly friends and stayed put in Caesarea, or was he correct in proceeding with his plans in the way that he did? Application is an important issue to get right.

One of the features which distinguish false prophecy from true is that the former pretends to an inspiration concerning knowledge which has been discovered by natural means (investigation, interrogation or intuition). It is also so vague and generalized as to be, like the horoscopes in the daily newspaper, applicable to large numbers of different people in entirely diverse circumstances. It is also so open-ended that nobody knows what should be done with it. In authentic prophecy we see revelation, interpretation, and application all combined with a truly God-given precision.

Elisha now operates prophetically as he speaks into the life of the Shunammite woman whose son he had raised to life some time before (2 Kings 4:8-37). The three elements of authentic prophecy are all here.

1. Revelation

"The LORD has decreed a famine." The prophet Amos stated, "Surely the LORD God does nothing without revealing his purpose to his servants the prophets" (Amos 3:7). God makes plans, but He loves to tell men and women His secrets, and then to commission them to broadcast those secrets until everybody who needs to know is also acquainted with them. In predicting a famine, Elisha was disclosing facts unrecognizable at the level of nature. Famine is a curse (Deut. 28:18, 23-24), and behind it lies the operation of spiritual forces hostile to man; forces which adversely affect the fertility of the seed and which also interfere with the conditions of both soil and environment. Whenever God removes His protection from a land then these forces of destruction are permitted to go to work (Rev. 6:8). Famine has an explanation in terms of the immediate causes involved—for example, drought, flood, or pestilence—but the real explanation is invariably spiritual and the ultimate cause is God. "The LORD has decreed a famine." Famine is one form of judgment upon sin. It is provoked by idolatry and immorality, the refusal of a nation to submit to God's Word and to obey it.

2. Interpretation

"A famine that will last seven years." This is very specific. There is nothing vague about this and it does not deal in generalities. Prophets can know what is coming in the future because that future is shaped by the all-controlling hands of God, the God Who is prepared to communicate His plans. Tozer says that the prophet's message "must alarm, arouse, challenge; it must be God's present voice to a particular people." That is exactly what we have here.

3. Application

"Go away with your family and stay for a while wherever you can." The people of God are warned of the famine and given a way out. (For a New Testament example of this see Agabus' prediction in Acts 11:28-30.) The prophet has opened a window in the Shunammite's closed world. He has brought the future into today and exhorted her to action in the light of that future. This is a major function of prophecy.

Now, the motive behind all this was God's desire to save and restore His people. Prompt obedience to prophetic words brings immense rewards. It is striking to see the woman's response. She obeyed and took action, not because she had seen the proof but because she believed the bare Word of God. As yet, there was no evidence of famine, yet she believed Elisha's testimony on the basis of the inward testimony of the Holy Spirit alone. Her reaction was prompt and unhesitating. She honored the prophetic word. Jesus said, "My sheep hear my voice" (John 10:3-4), and there is within every believer an instinctive recognition of the Lord's voice, combined with a desire to act upon what He says. The major difference, spiritually speaking at least, between the Lord's sheep and goats is that sheep don't "but!" Argumentativeness, hesitancy, and reluctance when God has clearly spoken may lead us into trouble. It is also noticeable that she and her family moved into Philistia, the home of Israel's traditional enemies since the time of the Judges. It is better to live in a cursed land under God's blessing than in the Promised Land under God's curse.

This was a faith-move for her and her family, and faith invariably entails both sacrifice and cost. We may well forfeit many things in obedience to Christ's commands. It will possibly entail the loss of our rights, our status, and even our property or belongings should we choose to do the will of God. It wasn't easy for the Shunammite as she became separated from her people, from the familiar religious privileges she had known and from her land. She took on the role of a resident alien in a threatening environment for the long spell of seven years. In her absence the family house and land were lost; either snatched by predatory squatters or confiscated by the king—illegal theft by robbers, or legalized theft by the state.

What the Shunammite received was justice, worked on her behalf by the God of justice. In the Bible justice is a key theme, particularly in the Prophets. Simply defined, justice means working out what belongs to whom and then returning it to them. There can be no credit to Joram in this act of redistribution of land, for God made him do it. God is fully aware of the calculating covetousness of modern economies and the rapacious taxing powers of the modern state and He is quite capable of guarding the rights of the marginalized and the weak. The woman stands as a paradigm or model for all who lie overwhelmed and helpless before the force of human pride vaunting its autonomy from God.

She also stands as a symbol of the church. Like her, we live in a kind of exile while our fellow citizens starve. Predatory agents have confiscated so much. We have been robbed of spiritual power, precious truth, much physical property, and even our faith. But God's plan is our restoration and as we believe God's prophets, we too will see how God goes to work on our behalf. The God of justice has worked out what belongs to whom and He will see that it is returned in full and with interest.

Upon her return to Israel at the end of the seven years she went to the king to plead her case for the recovery of what was rightfully hers. Humanly speaking this was a futile exercise. There was only a slim chance of success and the prospects were, if anything, even more grim than those which prevailed during her sojourn in Philistia. It was as though she was being penalized for her piety and paying dearly for her obedience. However, the day of divine intervention was not past, either for her or for us. She went to the king, the very same king who had at least permitted the illegal misappropriation of her property and may well also have been directly responsible for it. "The king's heart is in the hands of the Lord; He directs it like a watercourse wherever He pleases" (Prov. 21:1). It's great to know that God can intervene on our behalf even with the most potentially hostile and powerful adversary. We can see the restoration of all that we lost in difficult times. The woman's example assures us that it is right to go through the proper legal channels for the redress of wrongs, provided we are not motivated by greed, covetousness, or resentment—but what matters supremely is that you have God working on your behalf.

We call these things "coincidence," but coincidence is frequently the way God's providence operates. The woman approached the king just as the monarch was interviewing Gehazi,

Elisha's old aide, and sounding him out concerning the more exciting anecdotes of the prophet's astonishing ministry. You will recall
that Gehazi had been involved in the attempt to raise the
Shunammite's son from the dead, and it was doubtless because his
own efforts had failed so miserably that Gehazi could never forget
Elisha's astonishing success in seeing life re-enter the child's
motionless corpse. At any rate, Gehazi was telling the king about
the boy's resuscitation just at the moment when the woman came
in. Gehazi's jaw dropped and his eyes widened in astonished
surprise. "Why it's her! She's here . . . this is the boy's mother, my
lord, the one I'm telling you about . . . this is the lady whose son
died and whom Elisha helped that day! Ask her yourself . . . she'll
tell you it's all true!"

Without stopping to find out why she had come, the king
wanted to know about the miracle. No doubt she gave him a lot of
color and detail, describing the fields, the house, the annex she had
built for the prophet, and above all the amazing moment the boy
sneezed and started to breathe again. "What a coincidence!" we say.
"How lucky for her . . . the king wouldn't have given her the time
of day otherwise." No, not luck, not chance, and not coincidence.
This was a divine appointment and the king was so softened by her
story that he appointed one of his top officials to look into her
grievance. The result was that she had everything she had lost
restored with interest.

"Restored with interest." That will be the church's blessing
throughout the world in the years to come. We are more than
conquerors, and the evil one will be made to return everything he
has stolen from us, whether it was stolen directly or indirectly. It is
the ministry of the prophet to lead God's people out of their
bondage and into God's planned blessings. Hosea commented on
Moses' role in the deliverance of the Exodus in this way: "The
LORD used a prophet to bring Israel up from Egypt, by a prophet
he cared for him" (Hosea 12:13). Prophets light the way to full
restoration and the recovery of all that the church has lost down the

long centuries of her entanglement in the hostile environment of this world.

Lighting the fuse of divine retribution

Prophets also announce God's judgment upon the workings of sin both in individual lives and in societies. There is little fear of God today. This is partly because the church has toned down its teaching on divine retribution and has even apologized for the severity of God's acts recorded in the Bible. It is not our responsibility to vindicate God, for He is quite capable of vindicating Himself. Our responsibility is to speak the truth prophetically to our generation. The prophet Elisha now moves to unleash the chastening power of God.

Chastening takes three forms: first *internal chastening*, when God speaks to us by His Word and Spirit deep within our conscience, producing the discomfort of an uneasy and burdened conviction of sin. This is intended to shake us out of our lethargy and apathy. If this is not successful God moves to the second phase, *external chastening*, the experience of physical adversity. This may take the form of hardships, trials, persecutions, financial loss, accident, sickness, or rejection. The Bible prepares us for this. The writer to the Hebrews says, "My son, do not make light of the LORD's discipline, and do not lose heart when he rebukes you, because the LORD disciplines those he loves, and he punishes everyone he accepts as a son" (Heb. 12:5-6). In extreme cases God will resort to *terminal chastening*. Wayward believers may even die prematurely, their earthly existence suddenly terminated. This happened to Ananias and Sapphira for lying to the Holy Spirit in Acts 5, and it may be what Paul threatened should happen to the immoral brother at Corinth in 1 Corinthians 5:4-5.

Internal chastening had been the experience of the dynasty of Omri from the time of King Ahab onward, yet God's prophetic word to the nation of Israel through both Elijah and Elisha had largely gone unheeded. The next two incidents show us God "turning the screws" on the nation which refused to repent at His word. The people became candidates for external and terminal chastening.

1. External chastening

Elisha went to Damascus, and Ben-Hadad king of Aram was ill. When the king was told, "The man of God has come all the way up here," he said to Hazael, Take a gift with you and go to meet the man of God. Consult the LORD through him; ask him, 'Will I recover from this illness?'"

Hazael went to meet Elisha, taking with him as a gift forty camel-loads of all the finest wares of Damascus. He went in and stood before him, and said, "Your son Ben-Hadad king of Aram has sent me to ask, 'Will I recover from this illness?'"

Elisha answered, "Go and say to him, 'You will certainly recover'; but the LORD has revealed to me that he will in fact die." He stared at him with a fixed gaze until Hazael felt ashamed. Then the man of God began to weep.

"Why is my lord weeping?" asked Hazael.

"Because I know the harm you will do to the Israelites," he answered. "You will set fire to their fortified places, kill their young men with the sword, dash their little children to the ground, and rip open their pregnant women."

Hazael said, "How could your servant, a mere dog, accomplish such a feat?"

"The Lord has shown me that you will become king of Aram," answered Elisha.

Then Hazael left Elisha and returned to his master. When Ben-Hadad asked, "What did

Elisha say to you?" Hazael replied, "He told me that you would certainly recover." But the next day he took a thick cloth, soaked it in water and spread it over the king's face, so that he died. Then Hazael succeeded him as king (2 Kings 8:7-15).

Elisha moved north to the Aramean capital of Damascus, where he had been prophetically commissioned to prepare a scourge which God would use to beat the hide off the apostate nation of Israel. The Aramean king Ben-Hadad was lying in bed sick, and upon hearing of Elisha's excursion into Aramean territory the desperate king sent for a word from the prophet asking for the likely prognosis of his disease. He wanted to know if he would recover. Ben-Hadad had apparently been on reasonably friendly terms with Israel since the siege of Samaria when his armies were so mysteriously spooked by the supernatural auditory hallucination of the noise of a great defending army (see 2 Kings 7). It was to Israel's advantage for Ben-Hadad to remain alive so that the uneasy truce could be maintained.

Elisha was in Syrian territory on an altogether different errand. He was there to set in motion events which would lead to the death of Ben-Hadad and open the way for the succession of the brutal and ambitious Hazael—a figure who would pose a far more dangerous threat to Israel than the now benign but sickly Ben-Hadad.

It is interesting that in desiring to know whether or not he would recover from his illness Ben-Hadad did not send to the priests at the temple of Rimmon where he regularly worshiped. At this critical time he didn't want religion, certainly not sham religion, he wanted reality. The king knew that Elisha was a man who really heard from God, and he knew that the man of God had the capacity to confirm whether or not he would recover. I was once enabled to tell one of my critically ill church members that she would recover from her serious illness. I gave her the words Jesus spoke concerning his friend Lazarus, "This illness is not unto death." Miraculously she quickly recovered. Five years ago my own life hung in the balance through a long and serious illness which seemed at its lowest point to smash all hopes of recovery. More than one Christian leader stood at my hospital bedside and spoke with a certainty which I can never forget and which I could see was from God, to the effect that I would be healed and that God would preserve my life and restore my ministry. I am glad to say that they were right, and I thank God for the prophetic ability He gives to some, an ability which enables them to speak with such confidence concerning the outcome of life-threatening illness. In some cases they can even tell a person why they are sick and what God wants done about it.

Ben-Hadad was marked by a deep respect and honor for the visiting prophet. He didn't ask, "Have you any expenses, brother?", hoping the answer would be "No!" Rather he sent in advance of any ministry no fewer than forty camels and a vast selection of Syrian "goodies," the equivalent of a truck load or dockyard container of presents for the prophet. Not only that, he deferred to Elisha, thus honoring the man of God's position, referring to himself as "your son Ben-Hadad." Jesus said, "Anyone who receives a prophet because he is a prophet will receive a prophet's reward" (Matt. 10:41). The word Elisha gave was emphatic, "You will certainly recover," yet paradoxically Elisha knew at the same time that the king would die. The explanation was simple. The king would recover from certain death by "natural causes" only to die by "unnatural causes," namely, by the murderous hands of Hazael, the king's successor. Looking into Hazael's eyes that day, Elisha not only saw his murderous intent towards his sick monarch, he also saw the hatred which the Syrian bore for Israel. The prophet wept because he saw the sickening atrocities Hazael would perpetrate indiscriminately upon the inhabitants of each successive stronghold he would breach within Israel's borders.

So Ben-Hadad's condition was not terminal, but would prove to be so on account of Hazael's ambition. Some people are healed only to die. That is why healing should not be the only blessing men and women seek from God. Forgiveness and reconciliation with the LORD are the greatest favors God can give. With physical healing we may succeed in postponing for a while the death we are not yet ready to die, but with forgiveness, even if we are not healed, we are ready to die at any time. Better to die sick but forgiven than to die well only to face the judgment of God.

Elisha was deeply disturbed by what he saw. Prophets have powerful emotions and some of the insights, foresights, and words which they pass on are the occasion of genuine upset, embarrassment, or disturbance within the prophet's soul. Chastening is an issue which has to be addressed by God's prophets, but it is not a pleasant message to convey. Elisha saw beyond Hazael's courteous and civil outward appearance into the devious machinations of his mind. It takes a prophet to see evil while it still wears the uniform of lower rank and the appearance of gentleness, compassion, and culture. Elisha saw that Hazael was nothing less than a dirty bird of prey, a vulture perched menacingly on the crooked branch of his own filthy ambitions.

Nations are ruined by rulers of this breed. In our own century we have seen what avaricious and brutally ambitious men have done to nations like Russia, Germany, Japan, Iran, Iraq, and Uganda. If God chastens a nation at the hands of men like Hazael, then pity that nation! Even within our civilized, democratic Western societies too many individuals have come to power whose lives are characterized by lust, greed for gain, and a callous indifference to the value of human life. God sees all of this, and while He does not sanction any of it, He frequently allows such vile men to run their course so that by the blunt instrument of their homicidal rule sin may be exposed for all its ugliness and chastened appropriately. In response to Elisha's prediction, Hazael expressed shocked surprise and referred to himself as a "mere dog." Hazael meant that he was too harmless and of too low a station to carry out such deeds. History shows that many jackals, coyotes, hyenas, and even pampered poodles have risen to positions of power out of all proportion to their inherent talent or worth. They are frequently used by God as instruments of judgment and then judged themselves in return. (See Isaiah 10:5-9, 12, 15-16 for a prophetic prediction of this principle at work in the history of Assyria.)

Hazael returned to Ben-Hadad, delivered the good news that the illness from which the king suffered was not terminal, and then promptly suffocated the king. Hazael deserves some kind of appointment as the patron saint of the euthanasia lobby; he turned off the king's life-support system when there was every hope of survival, purely for reasons of convenience and expediency. Death is in God's hands to administer, so pity the seriously ill patients who have a Hazael (or his kind) at their bedside when there is a possibility of recovery. Hazael wished to play God and so terminated the king's life. People awake from comas, cancers do go into remission, divine healing may intervene, and space should be given for God to speak the Gospel into the lives of the dying. The man who would later advance to abortion and infanticide ("dash their children to the ground and rip open pregnant women"), began his career by an act of "mercy killing" in the premature murder of a sick old man, who would actually have recovered.

The prophet saw this and wept. The prophet saw that abortion, infanticide, and euthanasia belong to the same family of sins under the patriarchy of one. All the offspring carry its family likeness. It is called murder.

What is happening when lovers of death like Hazael come to power? God is letting loose the consequences of our sin, He is allowing the external chastening of an unrepentant people to take place, and when such a scourge is unleashed upon Israel or indeed upon any nation, then it is long overdue that the nation responds to that call.

Hazael faithfully carried out his commission. See 2 Kings 8:28 and the summary recorded at the end of the narrative:

> In those days the LORD began to reduce the size
> of Israel. Hazael overpowered the Israelites
> throughout their territory east of the Jordan in all
> the land of Gilead ... from Aroer by the Arnon
> Gorge through Gilead to Bashan (2 Kings 10:32).

If only Israel had read the indicators clearly and repented, but she did not. That is why God's dealings escalated in severity.

2. Terminal chastening

Terminal chastening occurs when God says "Enough!" and gives no more space to repent. This happened to Joram by the hands of the usurper Jehu. This is how Jehu was "ordained" for his ministry.

> The prophet Elisha summoned a man from the
> company of the prophets and said to him, "Tuck
> your cloak into your belt, take this flask of oil with
> you and go to Ramoth Gilead. When you get
> there, look for Jehu son of Jehoshaphat, the son of
> Nimshi. Go to him, get him away from his
> companions and take him into an inner room.
> Then take the flask and pour the oil in his head
> and declare, 'This is what the LORD says: I anoint
> you king over Israel.' Then open the door and run;
> don't delay!" So the young man, the prophet, went
> to Ramoth Gilead. When he arrived, he found the
> army officers sitting together. "I have a message for
> you, commander," he said.
> "For which of us?" asked Jehu.
> "For you, commander," he replied.
> Jehu got up and went into the house. Then the
> prophet poured the oil on Jehu's head and
> declared, "This is what the LORD, the God of

Israel, says: 'I anoint you king over the LORD's people Israel. You are to destroy the house of Ahab your master, and I will avenge the blood of my servants the prophets and the blood of all the LORD's servants shed by Jezebel. The whole house of Ahab will perish. I will cut off from Ahab every last male in Israel—slave or free. I will make the house of Ahab like the house of Jeroboam son of Nebat and like the house of Baasha son of Ahijah. As for Jezebel, dogs will devour her on the plot of ground at Jezrel, and no-one will bury her.'" Then he opened the door and ran (2 Kings 9:1-10).

All sin carries with it a mandatory death penalty, "For the wages of sin is death" (Rom. 6:23). Sin is disruptive, disintegrative, and divisive. It separates men and women from the source of wholeness and life because it alienates us from God. God in turn is utterly repulsed and revolted by the rebellion of His creatures and while He offers mercy, frequently for what seems an inordinately long space of time, there comes a day when that window of opportunity is decisively closed and God's mercy gives way to His wrath. The Lord then ratifies our choice to live within the realm of death by judicially consigning us to its clutches forever. The fate of the impenitent is to be consigned to a place of darkness, isolation, and torment forever. This place is called hell. It is a place of privative and punitive punishment described vividly under the metaphors of darkness and fire, where the Devil, his demons and all of their human co-conspirators against God's government will finally be consigned and contained for all eternity (Rev. 14:10; 20:10-18; 21:8).

Modern state powers and humanist thinkers are repelled by the whole concept of retributive punishment and consider the concept to be barbaric and unenlightened. Even many Christian thinkers are embarrassed by the sheer scale and menacing tones of the number of biblical texts which deal with the subject of divine retribution against sin. The doctrine of hell, as traditionally understood, has become an embarrassment to many contemporary theologians, Bible teachers, and ordinary Christians. Yet you will never understand the necessity or the true significance of the cross of Jesus unless you see it in terms of divine retribution against human sin. There the representative man, the last Adam, voluntarily yielded to the decision to absorb into Himself the due penalty against human autonomy, perversion, twistedness, and sin. Jesus carried the physical, psychic, and spiritual consequences of our sin. He endured physical death and the torments of hell itself. The ultimate penalty for sin is death, and Christ stood for us in order to carry the death penalty in our place. Jesus" death was not merely a martyrdom or an example of selfless love alone, it was the implementation of a judicial sentence which God's court had passed on the human race.

Sin is punished in one of two places—on the cross of Jesus where the God-man was hung for six indescribable hours of torture, torment, and misery, or in the lake of fire in hell forever. You and I choose for ourselves where our own penalty will be administered. By God's grace millions have already decided to elect for Jesus to stand as substitute for them, and by faith they have been released from the prospect of hell. They are forgiven. An amnesty has been granted by God Himself.

The fact remains, however, that untold multitudes defiantly opt to remain outlaws from God's orderly kingdom. Born in hostility against His benevolent rule, they choose to remain in angry rebellion until the day of their death. They may flirt with religion and even cultivate a "spirituality" of some sort, but it will be a piety on their own terms, tailored to their own perceived needs, a homespun belief system which refuses divine revelation and enthrones human rationality. Even at their most religious, men and women can be at their most rebellious, for false religion is the most explicit proof that we are at war with God—it wants some sort of god but not the living God.

The dynasty of Omri in the northern kingdom of Israel was at war with God. At last, God issued the death warrant on its vaunted independence and rule. Elisha commissioned a deputy prophet to visit one of King Joram's commanders, Jehu. This prophet would carry out the divine sentence upon the royal family. By this action Elisha prophetically fired the fuse of divine retribution against the sins of the ruling household. Political and religious corruption were finally to be dealt with; internal and external chastening at last gave way to terminal chastening. The morally and spiritually polluted descendants of Ahab and Jezebel were to be terminated, along with the priests and worshipers of the demon-god Baal (see 2 Kings 9-10).

The wrath of God is revealed from heaven against all the ungodliness and unrighteousness of men (Rom. 1:18). All false religion with its attendant corrupt lifestyles will encounter its nemesis; its reckoning day will come. The ancient Canaanite deities of Mammon, Baal, and Molech, are still worshiped today, albeit under different names. We call them "Money," "Sex," and "Power." Wherever you see people bound by the pursuit of riches, twisted by the indulgence of illicit sensual experience or obsessed with the idea of the personal control of other people, then you are seeing powerful demonic forces at work. God is at war with all unclean contenders against His kingdom of trust, purity, and servanthood. He will judge the modern expressions of Baalism just as surely as He judged its ancient manifestations in the ninth century B.C. If we too are greedy for gain, obsessed with perversion and guilty of the devaluation of human life then the sentence of death hangs over us, just as menacingly as it hung over the descendants of Omri.

Jehu became God's instrument of punishment, and he was "ordained" by the prophet to fulfill this "ministry" of vengeance and divine retribution. Read the narrative and you will see that Jehu's friends thought that the prophet was crazy. Because of this they were disinclined to believe anything he had said in his exchange with Jehu, but nevertheless when Jehu reported the announcement that he was to be Joram's successor and the founder of a new dynasty within Israel, these men knew immediately that this prediction was true and paid homage to their new monarch.

> When Jehu went out to his fellow officers, one of them asked him, "Is everything all right? Why did this madman come to you?"
>
> "You know the man and the sort of things he says," Jehu replied.
>
> "That's not true!" they said. "Tell us."
>
> Jehu said, "Here is what he told me: 'This is what the LORD says: I anoint you king over Israel.'"
>
> They hurried and took their cloaks and spread them under him on the bare steps. Then they blew the trumpet and shouted, "Jehu is king!" (2 Kings 9:11-13).

A terrible bloodbath followed, in which Jehu, Ahaziah (king of Judah), the aging witch Jezebel, and numerous descendants of Ahab all died brutal and bloody deaths. In the same way, the ministers and priests of the state-funded cult of Baal were all tricked into attending a service at the palace and were butchered also. Emerson once said, "The frost which kills the harvest of a year, saves the harvest of a century by destroying the weevil or the locust." God's judgment is always right, always just. It purges destructive forces from both individuals and whole societies. The Judge of all the earth does right.

The Bible says that "without the shedding of blood there can be no remission of sin" (Heb. 9:22). The shedding of blood cleanses. The most powerful detergent in the whole of the universe is the blood of God's Son; refuse that blood, however, and you will shed your own; for God is determined to eradicate the pollution of sin from His universe. Blood must be shed if sin is to be covered and God will accept only one of two significant blood-sheddings to cover your sin; it will either be your own blood which will be shed for all eternity in hell (your blood will never fully atone for your sin—sin is that serious), or it will be the blood of Jesus which satisfied God's justice once and for all when it was spilled so violently on the cross. Prophets are called to announce and repeatedly reiterate these solemn truths. It is not an enviable responsibility in an age so soft and decadent in its self-indulgent orgy of sin. But God will clean up His world one way or another— either by retribution or restoration. The prophetic word is God's primary agency in the initiation of both.

That's why we must ask the question: "Is there a prophet in the house?"

1. Philip Greenslade *Leadership—Patterns for Biblical Leadership Today* (Marshalls: Basingstoke, 1984), pp. 145-146.
2. William H. Willimon *Peculiar Speech* (Wm. B. Eerdmans: Grand Rapids, 1992), p. 86.

OUR VICTORY IN DEATH

15

2 Kings 13:14-21

> Now Elisha was suffering from the illness from
> which he died. Jehoash king of Israel went down
> to see him and wept over him. "My father! My
> father!" he cried. "The chariots and horsemen of
> Israel!" (2 Kings 13:14).

Elisha was ill—terminally ill. "Now Elisha was suffering from the
illness from which he died." And so the narrator has skipped many
intervening laps in Elisha's long race with the baton of spiritual
anointing which he had seized from Elijah, to bring us, in effect,
directly to the last few hundred miles and the finishing tape. Elisha
began his race by a clear identification with God and with God's
leader by following Elijah across the Jordan. He also experienced
an anointing with the power of God's Holy Spirit. For us today this
stands as equivalent to proper initiation into the Christian life by
baptism in water and baptism in the Spirit. Elisha's life was marked
at the outset by surrender to the will of God at whatever cost (see
1 Kings 19:19-21). He then followed his master in total loyalty
even when he was criticized or questioned for doing so (2 Kings
2:2). He refused to settle for half-measures and claimed a double

portion of Elijah's anointing, an empowering which was evident to all (2 Kings 2:9, 15). From then on his course was marked by continued fruitfulness right to the end. There is no record that Elisha ever complained against God or ran from his enemies. He never failed in courage or lapsed into immorality. He remained a faithful man of prayer marked by deep sensitivity to the prompting of the Spirit. By far the majority of his miracles were healings and works of restoration. God's love and grace shone through him. This is what it means to be filled with the Spirit. The Puritan William Gurnall said, "Whenever you meet a Christian you meet a man who is on his way to heaven." This is the distinguishing feature of a believer. We are headed somewhere, and the glow of that goal irradiates our lives at every point on the journey.

We are going to consider Elisha's death. He died well. Back in the eighteenth century the Methodist leader John Wesley said that one of the great testimonials to the truth of his message and the caliber of his work was the fact, as he put it, that "our people die well!" True freedom is freedom from the fear of death. You are not ready to live until you are first ready to die. Loyalty to God means that you will be willing to lay down your life in whatever way He says in order to win the war. If you are not willing to die, then the Devil will be permitted to have some kind of hold over you. You will never win any battle in which you are more anxious to save your own skin than to save the day for the Lord's cause.

The need for heroes

Centuries before, the wayward prophet Balaam prayed, "Let me die the death of the righteous and may my end be like theirs" (Num. 23:10). It will be profitable to look at the end of Elisha's career. It is a fine conclusion and epilogue to a life which has served to encourage and inspire us at every turn.

Lives are meant to do that. They are meant to inspire. It is right to have heroes and heroines. The problem with men and women today is that they are choosing the wrong heroes. They are listening to the wrong stories. Some choose to copy the empty and trivial life of a rock or movie star. Even a U.S. president commended Sylvester Stallone's character *Rambo* as an inspiration to the American public. As a boy I used to collect bubble gum picture cards of soccer stars like Jimmy Greaves, Bobby Charlton, and Ian St. John. They are all balding and bulging in the wrong places now. They are well past their prime. You may never have heard of them. That is what the passage of time does.

This is a good reason why our greatest models and heroes should be those listed in the Bible. There is a timeless quality about them. The stories of men like Abraham, Moses, Joshua, David, Elijah, Elisha, Amos, Jeremiah, or Paul have the power to elevate and to ennoble us as few other stories can. We act as though comfort and luxury are the chief requirements of life when all that we really need to make us truly happy is something to get us excited, something that will grip us and see us right through to the end. The Bible is full of men and women who had just such a purpose and goal. Elisha, as we have seen, was no exception.

Such saints teach us that if you are a man or woman of destiny then your destiny will not desert you at the point of your final departure. This sense of vocation is what sustains the Christian life up to and beyond the point of death. It is what explains the credibility of so many Christians and Christian leaders. Much Christian leadership today is passing through a credibility crisis. Disappointment and disillusionment with fallen leaders have led many to ask with increasing urgency of each new successor who arrives to head up a church or mission, "Can I trust this person?" Usually that question breaks down into several components. We saw this in an earlier chapter. Credibility is established by at least three different inquiries, all of which require an affirmative answer. I am now going to add a fourth to our list.

1. Does he know what he is talking about?—the issue of *expertise*.
2. Do I like him?—the issue of charisma or *personality*.
3. Can I trust him?—the issue of *trustworthiness*.
4. Has he been tested over time?—the issue of *durability*.

Elisha is credible on all four grounds, not least the test of durability. He endured to the end. He was still serving as God's man right to the very end. Let's see what we can learn from this. This brief narrative yields at least four principles. Let's consider them as we notice Elisha's last appearance.

Like Elisha, you and I can die in God's perfect timing

The annals of church history are punctuated with the stories of some of God's choicest servants who died prematurely, at least by our reckoning. Men like David Brainerd, Henry Martyn, and Robert Murray McCheyne all died young. In our own generation we have lamented the loss of Jim Elliot, Keith Green, and the late Canon David Watson of York. It seems that they all died too soon. It is bound to look like that if you have a stunted view of the sovereignty of God, but if God is truly sovereign then we acknowledge that He alone can determine the day of our death. Hence, we are all immortal until our life's work is done.

Statistically speaking, 100 percent of all people die. You cannot choose whether or not you will die, but you can choose how you will be living when you die. You can choose on whose side you will be fighting when you die.

Elisha lay dying from an unnamed terminal illness. He was about to go home to God by a somewhat less royal route than that taken by Elijah. Elijah was "raptured" alive to heaven by special limousine—a fiery chariot. He thus stands as a type of all those who will be alive in Christ at the return of the Lord. They will be lifted or "snatched" from the earth without dying (1 Thes. 4:17). Elisha went by the more ordinary route reserved for all generations of believers but the last one; the way of physical disintegration and death. His body wasted away, his breathing became shallow, his strength failed, and his bodily processes began to malfunction. All the things we dread about dying were experienced by Elisha. We tend to postpone thinking about such disintegration until we are forced to, and even then we hope we'll be drugged and removed from its worst realities. "There is none so old but thinks he may live a little longer, and though in general we say 'All must die,' yet in the false numbering of his own particular days he thinks to live forever" (Nehemiah Rogers). Or in the words of another Puritan, "The long habit of living indisposes us for dying" (Thomas Browne).

The moment we came into this world we began to go out of it. Every day we live brings us a day nearer to our death. Such a sobering thought is worth serious consideration, for it helps us to assess the quality of life we live now and the thoroughness of preparation we have made for the end of it. It is possible to have no real anxiety at all when we come to that last great crisis. The apostle Paul said, "None of us lives to himself alone, and none of us dies to himself alone. . . . If we live, we live to the LORD; and if we die, we die to the LORD. So, whether we live or die, we belong to the LORD" (Rom. 14:7-8). If you are presently living in the LORD then you will die in the LORD. The timing and mode of departure will be just right. Death for a believer is comparatively unimportant. Death may look terrible from a distance, but when we get up close to it Christ will have altered its complexion considerably. The horror has been taken out of it by Jesus' own death for us. He has promised to walk with us through the experience each step of the way. You will not walk alone if you belong to Christ. The great Bible commentator Matthew Henry put it like this, "He whose head is in heaven need not fear to put his feet into the grave." For us, as for Elisha, death was but a temporal incident in an immortal career.

Like Elisha, you and I can look back on a job well-done and a life well-lived

It was a touching death-bed scene. The king Jehoash came to pay his last respects. Jehoash, the grandson of Jehu, is part of a long line of kings who interlace the narrative of the books of Kings. He was a formally legitimate heir to the throne but scandalously illegitimate in much of his conduct and behavior. This explains why his life was inconsequential in terms of Israel's faith and history and therefore why his deeds are recorded in a few lines and are not worthy of reflection, whereas Elisha's deeds occupy long sections of narrative. Jehoash was the ostensible leader but barely left a trace of his presence. The same cannot be said of Elisha. That is why the king visited the prophet when the latter was on his death bed.

It is extremely thought-provoking to listen to the exchange which takes place between these two men. Jehoash was clearly moved at the sight of the dying prophet. He could not help acknowledging Elisha's true worth to the nation. "My father! My father! . . . The chariots and horsemen of Israel!" In these words Jehoash not only expressed his own personal sense of grief, but he acknowledged the loss to his country. The prophet had been the nation's best defense and his departure would leave an enormous breach in the invisible spiritual walls protecting his kingdom. This is true for the church today. Our presence as God's people within our nation is the most significant factor in the welfare of our country. Years ago Geoffrey King said, "To be a Christian is to be a key person in the world situation today." We need to view ourselves in the light of that statement.

In this beautiful yet curious narrative we cannot escape reiterating the conclusion that in God's estimation it is prophetic people who really do shape history. Jehoash was shamelessly acknowledging how dependent he was on the prophet. The well-being of a kingdom depends upon the active presence and power of God's prophetic people, and even the king knows it. The little kingdoms and political domains of this world need the sustenance and active intervention of God's great kingdom which comes from another realm altogether. The church is here as the agent of that other kingdom.

God has made us ambassadors of another empire. We carry a message that can affect the destinies of both men and nations. Elisha knew that, and so as he lay dying from the only illness that we know he ever suffered from, he could look back upon a life over which both God and men could record the verdict "Mission Accomplished." There isn't a hint of pain, regret, remorse, or the haunting memory of failure.

In one sense, then, your whole life has been the preparation for your end. When you come to die, it is good to have nothing else left to do other than to die. It is a fine retrospect to be able to say that you have "run the race and finished the course" (cf. 2 Tim. 4:6-7). Your career as a husband or wife, father or mother, laborer or business person, Christian leader, or disciple should be viewed with a deep sense of accomplishment. Every life is a profession of faith of some kind or other and exercises an inevitable and silent influence. What was yours?

Elisha exemplified the promise of Proverbs 4:18, "The path of the righteous is like the first gleam of dawn, shining ever brighter till the full light of day." We are meant to go out at the noonday of our influence and not at the sunset. If you live that kind of life you won't depart either in gloom or into gloom. "Take care of your life and the Lord will take care of your death" (George Whitefield). Elisha is a spur and incentive to this kind of living, for he was never a soul consumed with self and therefore wrapped up in sourness and misery. He was a "live-for-others" type of individual who made it his chief aim to do the will of God. "The man who does the will of God lives for ever" (1 John. 2:17). God isn't here to rubber-stamp our decisions or to endorse our plans. We are here to align ourselves with His.

During the American Civil War, a deputation came to

Abraham Lincoln and asked him, "Are you sure that the Lord is on your side?" His reply shocked them. He said, "That is not the thing that I am most concerned about." His hearers were astounded—what could be more important to a pious leader during a time of war than whether or not God is on his side? Lincoln explained, "What I am most anxious about is whether or not we are on the Lord's side." Fear God and you will have nothing less to fear, not even death.

Like Elisha, you and I can be a blessing to others even on our death beds

> Elisha said, "Get a bow and some arrows," and he did so. "Take the bow in your hands," he said to the king of Israel. When he had taken it, Elisha put his hands on the king's hands.
>
> "Open the east window," he said, and he opened it. "Shoot!" Elisha said, and he shot. "The LORD's arrow of victory, the arrow of victory over Aram!" Elisha declared. "You will completely destroy the Arameans at Aphek" (2 Kings 13:15-17).

A life lived for others is a loving life. A life filled with love will be a life free of fear. And so Elisha is here seen devoid of the fear of death and still lovingly concerned for the welfare of the king and the nation. What is this business with the arrows all about?

It is a symbolic action. Elisha was symbolically urging God's people to victory over God's enemies. Elisha was being removed from the scene of battle but the fight would still go on. A picture emerges of a man whose heart was still alive to the issues of the hour, and who was still capable of feeling stirred to action. Elisha knew where the real enemy lay and where the fight was to be taken.

We see him stirring others to that fight. The prophet was no longer capable of pulling a bow himself, but he could still lay hands upon the hands that could. He was conveying anointing on Jehoash's hands. He was trying to stir up the sluggish, compromised young king with some enthusiasm to fight the enemy. The prowess, skill, and administration of royalty can guarantee nothing, least of all victory over powerful and malevolent forces bent on destruction. The true source of victory lies elsewhere. The prophet knows where victory comes from and in that knowledge he both knows more and can do more than the king. History is full of strange victories. Who knows why one side wins and another lies vanquished on the field of battle?

> There is no wisdom, no insight, no plan
> that can succeed against the LORD.
> The horse is made ready for the day of battle,
> but victory rests with the LORD (Prov. 21:30-31).

It is clear from such examples as the Battle of Britain, Dunkirk, D-Day, the Korean and Vietnam wars, or the more recent troubles in Northern Ireland, the Middle East, and parts of Africa that victory is not always decided by rational scientific planning and superior weapon power. There is more going on than military strategists and informed observers can see.

Elisha overflowed with faith. He spoke with confidence of an outcome that was certain in his own mind. Aram would be completely defeated. We are left with the impression that Jehoash was only very reluctantly caught up in Elisha's final flush of prophetic anointing. It seems that the king may have complied somewhat patronisingly in order to try and humor the "delirious" old man. Even so, Jehoash must surely have felt some sparks from the fire of the old boy's faith, because in the next instant Elisha commands him to shoot some of his quiverful of arrows into the ground.

We now see Elisha rebuking unbelief. Jehoash meekly complied with phase two of the prophetically directed action.

> Then he said, "Take the arrows," and the king took them. Elisha told him, "Strike the ground." He struck it three times and stopped. The man of God was angry with him and said, "You should have struck the ground five or six times; then you would have defeated Aram and completely destroyed it. But now you will defeat it only three times" (2 Kings 13:18-19).

He meekly fired three arrows into the dusty earth around the prophet's bed. Why didn't he fire the whole quiverful by faith? Why didn't he get excited and let fly with six or seven arrows into the dusty floor beneath the bed? This was a mock battle that would have predicted the outcome of the real thing. Why not let fly with all he had at his disposal?

Perhaps he felt silly. It's possible he didn't have a clue what was going on. Much more likely, however, is the interpretation Elisha gave. Jehoash simply didn't believe it. He didn't believe there could be any connection between firing arrows in privacy and later seeing total victory in public. God has exactly the same trouble with us in regard to prayer. We limp in our prayer lives. We struggle to believe that a few words launched from our knees at a bedside in private can achieve anything in the "real world" out there in the public arena. We don't get angry enough with God's enemies. We don't act decisively enough at God's prophetic prompting and like Jehoash we don't pray persistently enough to see the breakthrough come. We feel silly. We don't understand. Quite simply, we don't believe. So we give up after two or three attempts.

Some answers to prayer come like torpedoes, but as Colin Urquhart said, "Some answers to prayer come like tortoises— slowly but surely." That is why we must not give up, for unbelief can stop the answer in its tracks. A half-won fight is one in which faith has lost ground to some form of unbelief. This can occur in many ways.

1. Skepticism can limit God's power

Jesus "could not do any miracles there . . . and he was amazed at their lack of faith" (Mark 6:5-6). It was not due to their small numbers, old buildings, or hard pews, but simply due to their skeptical cynicism that Jesus was prevented from working.

2. A low expectation limits God's power

Jehoash did not expect to conquer fully and so he did not totally "take out" the Syrians. If you believe you can do it, it is often nine-tenths done. Refuse to say "impossible" if God has told you to do it. With God all things are possible.

3. Small desire limits God's power

Did Jehoash have any stomach for this fight? Did he want to see Syria defeated? We have reason to doubt it. Similarly Jesus asked the cripple at Bethsaida, "Do you want to get well?" (John 5:6) and on another occasion He asked two blind men, "What do you want me to do for you?" (Matt. 20:32). These are vital questions. Most times we have not because we ask not. We are about as full of the Spirit as we want to be. We have the kind of church life we desired and asked for. A sobering thought, isn't it?

And yet conversely, it is also true that using your power increases your power. If you have a quiverful of arrows, why fire only three? If you have the instrument of prayer, why make small, paltry requests? "Whoever has will be given more; whoever does not have, even what he has will be taken from him" (Mark 4:25). If you let an ability or gift lie idle for too long it may atrophy. Hindu "holy men" lift their hands aloft until the arm withers and dies through lack of circulation. We have to use what we've got before we'll get more. We cannot wait for more faith when Jesus tells us bluntly to use the faith we have (Luke 17:6)! You can store grain in an unventilated granary where mold and rats will consume it, or you can sow it generously in a field and you'll reap a harvest.

Let's learn to ask and keep on asking. Don't give up after three tries when God is looking for five or six. Real faith is persevering faith. It will not take "no" for an answer. There are some enemies we have to smite repeatedly until they are utterly defeated. No wonder Elisha rebuked Jehoash. The king could get more worked up over a fast buck than a slow victory; over instant success than sustained assault. Faith will make us resolve to keep fighting, and especially in prayer. God will not bypass the instrumentality of prayer. As someone once said, "Prayer is not just part of the work, prayer is the work . . . the rest is just mopping up."

One last thing appears in the epilogue to this astonishing narrative.

Like Elisha, you and I can go on being a blessing even when we're gone

> Elisha died and was buried. Now Moabite raiders
> used to enter the country every spring. Once while
> some Israelites were burying a man, suddenly they
> saw a band of raiders, so they threw the man's body
> into Elisha's tomb. When the body touched
> Elisha's bones, the man came to life and stood up
> on his feet (2 Kings 13:20-21).

If you think of the legacy of the influence of men like Rousseau, Darwin, Nietzsche, or Marx, you will agree that these figures go on ministering death long after they are gone. They have cursed the world with the twisted systems of falsehood spawned from their angry and God-denying minds.

Even the narrator cannot turn loose his fascination with Elisha. We feel the same. That is why we should feel gratified that history records one last detail in the life of our history-maker. Even after death Elisha is not finished. "As a dead man he continues to live. As a dead man he continues to matter more than many persons ostensibly alive" (Walter Brueggemann). We may find it unsettling to see an incident of this sort recorded in sober historical narrative, but we must be challenged continuously to see history as God sees it.

This incident, amazing as it is, has been recorded in a succinct, matter-of-fact manner to teach us something of the dynamic, life-giving influence which men and women can impart long after they are dead. Elisha finally died. They didn't cremate him (a mode of disposal of the earthly remains of believers never favored in Scripture), but rather carefully buried his corpse in a tomb with an open entrance. In time the body decomposed leaving just bones, perhaps with a few tattered remnants of leather and cloth to signify that it had once been the body of God's servant Elisha.

Then a seemingly chance occurrence took place. Some Israelites were burying the body of an Israelite in the vicinity of Elisha's tomb. They had planned a proper and decent burial with full honors but at that time surprise raids were carried out by marauding bands of Moabites who invaded Israelite territory in the hunt for food and other plunder. The burial party was interrupted and instead of the planned proceedings they ended up unceremoniously dumping the body of their friend in Elisha's tomb. Sad development for them, but a terrific idea for their deceased friend! For at a time when you would think that nothing of Elisha's influence remained, nothing but his bones that is, they all found out that this was far from the case. A touch from the relics of Elisha was enough to resuscitate the Israelite and he came back from the dead. He stepped out of Elisha's tomb and presumably evaded the Moabite raiders also, since he lived long enough to tell the tale.

Medieval Catholicism has always valued relics of dead saints for similar reasons. By the time of the Reformation, this had become a traffic of such amazing corruption and appalling superstition that the Protestant Reformers like Calvin rightly reacted with scathing denunciation and biting sarcasm. For instance, in a piece published in 1544 on the "Relics of the Saints," Calvin says he knew that certain clergy

> pretend to have the manger, cradle, swaddling-clothes, foreskin and blood of Christ; the water-pots that were at the marriage of Cana; the wine into which Christ turned the water; the utensils and furniture that were used at the last supper; the manna of the children of Israel; the cross, cave, nails, sponge, lance, crown of thorns, coat, handkerchief, and tears of Christ; the milk, smock, hair, girdle, slipper, comb, and ring of the Virgin Mary; the dagger and buckler of Michael, the Archangel; the skull, jaw bone, brains and finger of John the Baptist; the chair, crosier, mass-attire, and brain of St. Peter; besides the bodies of the saints which were to be seen in several places, and yet are supposed to be one and the same.

Along with Calvin we can have no truck with superstition of this kind which attributes spiritual power to physical objects (fake or authentic) without the authorization of God.

Yet biblically speaking, it would appear that in certain exceptional cases God so chooses to honor the ministry and even the memory of certain men that He allows the anointing of His Spirit to accompany even physical objects associated with them. In Acts 19:11, "God did extraordinary miracles through Paul, so that even handkerchiefs and aprons that had touched him were taken to the sick, and their illnesses were cured and the evil spirits left them." During the public ministry of Jesus a woman who had suffered gynecological problems, with almost continuous menstrual bleeding for twelve years, was instantly healed simply by touching the tassels of Jesus' rabbinical robe (see Mark 5:24-34), and perhaps most astonishing of all was the way in which God used even Peter's shadow to endorse the reality of the anointing resting upon his apostolic ministry (Acts 5:12-16). There are some men and women God loves to own and to be identified with, even long after their deaths. This being so, why shouldn't Elisha's bones be used to raise the dead if God so chooses?

It is witness to the fact that Elisha is still alive. When God imparts His life to us, since the life of God can never die then we can never die. Elisha is alive on the other shore and God was prepared to endorse that fact. God vindicated His servant's ministry. He affirmed the fact that his message did not die along with him; indeed, that Elisha himself did not die along with his body. This is what one commentator calls "post-mortem corroboration of his undying influence." If you think about that even for one moment, then you have to conclude that you wouldn't mind a little of that also.

Cynics talk about the futility of life. "The evil that men do lives after them, the good is oft interred with their bones." This incident with Elisha's bones assures us that this is not always so. There is a kind of law of the conservation of spiritual energy—God continues to use us after we're gone. The most popular Christian author in the world today is the Victorian Baptist preacher C. H. Spurgeon, who died in 1892! People are still being converted through his printed sermons and other writings. What a legacy!

People may remember your life, words, or example. I remember reading the remarkable story of Luke Short. He was an Englishman who had emigrated to the United States in the late eighteenth century. He was converted at the age of 103 years. This happened while he was meditating under a tree in Virginia one hot afternoon, recalling a sermon he'd heard preached by the great Puritan John Flavel, back in Plymouth when he was a boy. That was over ninety years before, since Flavel died in 1791. Three years after his conversion, Luke Short died. On his gravestone there is this epitaph:

Here lies the body of Luke Short,
Aged according to nature 106 years,
Aged according to grace 3 years.

Now there's "post-mortem corroboration" for you!

I have frequently enjoyed reading the reprinted classics of the sixteenth-, seventeenth-, eighteenth- and nineteenth-century "prophets," the great spokesmen of God in former generations. Some scathingly call these older works "dead men's bones." They may well be the remains of dead men, but it has been my experience that I have been resuscitated by dead men's remains many times, and I have seen the same thing happen to others too. It can be said of them as it was said of Abel, "By faith he still speaks even though he is dead" (Heb. 11:4).

Funeral services are not my favorite events, yet I have been present at the funerals of many outstanding men and women of God. It has been so moving to listen to tributes and testimonies related to the influence of those lives, and on rare occasions I have known individuals who have been converted as a direct result of the anointing present at such a service. One man I knew was converted at the crematorium! It's that "resurrection energy overcoming the blight and downdrag of death" (Sidlow-Baxter) and we can only thank God for it.

This explains the poignancy of Balaam's prayer: "Let me die the death of the righteous and may my end be like theirs."

We leave Elisha's bones in their influential grave, but not before we take the example of his life and death to pose one more challenging question. Will the world be any different because you and I were born? Will things change because you lived and died doing the will of God?

All the world's great philosophers, gurus, and religious leaders can say at their most affirmative, "I was alive, and behold I am dead forever and ever." But Jesus said, "I was dead, and behold I am alive forever and ever!" (Rev. 1:18).

If you are connected with Jesus and alive with His Spirit then this can be your testimony too.

Like Elisha, in life and in death, we can show the world that God saves. As C. T. Studd says,

> Let us not rust out. Let us not glide through this world and then slip quietly out of it without having blown the trumpet loud and long for our Blessed Redeemer. At the very least, let us see to it that when the Devil gets news of our departure from the battlefield, he throws a thanksgiving party in hell!

PERSONAL & GROUP STUDY GUIDE

Chapter 1
Elijah Passes the Baton

1. Elijah was a prophet at a wicked period in Israel's history. He faced idol worship, child sacrifices, and wicked governments. What wickedness do we face in our world today?
2. Elijah became discouraged and disillusioned with his country and perhaps even with God. Why is it easy sometimes to lose sight of our purpose in Christ when we live in such an evil society?
3. Haslam compares generations to a relay race. Each generation runs its leg of the race, then passes off the baton to the next generation. What were the strengths of the generation before you in terms of how they lived their faith and affected the world?
4. What have been the strengths and weaknesses of your generation in carrying the influence of faith?
5. If God already knows the outcome of the race, how much does each of our individual parts of the race matter?
6. Elijah nearly dropped the baton (or failed). Think of a time when you've nearly dropped the baton, or actually dropped it. What helped you pick it up and start running again?
7. Read 1 Corinthians 12:7-11. We each have a gift that makes us a valuable part of the relay race of church history. What gifts do you see at work around you?
8. What signs of relativism (there is no absolute truth) are evident in your community?

9. Read Exodus 20:1-4, the beginning of the Ten Commandments. God commanded us to have no other gods, but rather to worship Him only. What other gods are prevalent in our culture today?
10. Elisha stepped forward to show his world that God not only is, but that He saves. How can we step forward to show our world that same thing?

Prayer Focus: Praise God for His ultimate victory over evil. Ask for strength to pass your own baton by sharing Christianity with your family.

Chapter 2
I'll Give You a Call Sometime

1. Name some ways our lives can show both God's power and His compassion.
2. In what ways have you been called of God?
3. What gives you the most joy in your service for God?
4. How can we discern which of our dreams or goals are simply our dreams and which are God's call manifesting itself in our lives?
5. Describe someone you know who is living out the call of God on his or her life.
6. Boreham is quoted as saying, "We make our decisions and then our decisions turn round and make us." How have you seen this in your own life?
7. How would Elijah's actions have been different if he felt as if *he* was calling Elisha, rather than God?
8. Elisha sacrificed the tools of his former trade to follow Elijah. What sacrifices have you or someone you love been asked to make for the sake of God's call?
9. Why is it easier to be a "sensation" rather than a "servant"?

10. What are the rewards of following God's call, even if the role He has for you is a background role with no attention or accolades from others?

Prayer Focus: We are all like Elisha, common, working people. But we are all called by God as well. Pray and ask God to formulate His call in your life, or affirm what He has already called you to. Acknowledge His power in your call.

Chapter 3
Be Prepared

1. Think of a time when you had to wait for something that you wanted very much. What words describe your feelings during that period?
2. Why is it difficult sometimes to trust God during our times of preparation?
3. Elisha was deeply committed to Elijah. Describe someone in your life to whom you feel deeply committed and would stand by even in difficult times.
4. So often we feel called by God to do something but give up on that call for reasons based only on other people and ourselves. What makes us switch focus?
5. Why is it often lonely to be a leader?
6. Describe a time when God surprised you or someone you know by doing something unexpected.
7. List some risks that could be involved with following God's call on your life.
8. How do you know when you are ready to take leadership?
9. The cloak, or mantle, was a symbol of power and authority. What symbols do we have today that would be similar?
10. What kinds of things hold you back from going full force toward God's call in your life?

Prayer Focus: Thank God for the trials that will develop perseverance in your ministry.

Chapter 4
Pollution Busters

1. Haslam states, "Our ecological crisis is at root a *moral* crisis." Do you agree or disagree? Why?
2. If God's wisdom is the truest and purest wisdom, what keeps Christians from being called upon to give advice on more of the earth's issues?
3. Haslam called Elisha a "thermostat rather than a thermometer" because Elisha changed his environment rather than reflecting it. What traits does it take to be a thermostat?
4. Read Matthew 5:13. Discuss the difference salt makes in our world. What keeps us as Christians from being that kind of seasoning and preserving agent?
5. Elisha helped make something bitter and corrupt into something sweet and useful. Name some bitter and corrupt places that you would like to influence for the good.
6. *Niceness* is not listed as a fruit of the Spirit, and yet as Christians we often expect each other to be nice all the time. What are some other expectations we place on each other that God never ordained an earmarks of a Christian?
7. When the young men teased Elisha it was an expression of contempt for the authority of God. What contempt for God's authority do we see today?
8. If you were given a five-minute platform to speak against an evil in our world, what would you speak against?
9. What are two things you can do this week about the moral pollution in your heart?
10. What are two things you can do this week about the moral and/or physical pollution in your community?

Prayer Focus: Pray for spiritual boldness and authority in your home, workplace, church, and community. Yearn for a worldwide revival that will heal evil through Christ.

Chapter 5
A Tale of Three Kings

1. Joram used some pick-and-choose tactics to decide which evils he would do away with and which he would incorporate. What are evidences in our world of picking and choosing the sins we will tolerate?
2. What could Joram have done differently in making his agreements with the other two kings that might have saved him some regret when they and their armies were suffering in the desert?
3. When Joram's plan was failing, he finally looked to God for answers. Think of a time when you were in a similar situation, asking God to help you out of circumstances that you brought on yourself. What factors cause us to ignore God at decision-making time, but cling to Him in trouble?
4. Part of Elisha's credibility was that he had spent time with Elijah. Who are some people that you hope will "rub off" on you the same way that Elijah rubbed off on Elisha?
5. What kinds of things keep us from speaking out boldly to the leadership in our communities and states?
6. Elisha used music to get in touch with God's Spirit. What helps you get in touch with God's Spirit?
7. God does perform miracles, but often we must do our part, digging ditches, as Joram had to. Name some tasks in today's church that would be "ditch-digging" tasks.
8. What are the best tools to use in spiritual warfare?
9. Who or what are some of the enemies of faith today?

Prayer Focus: Lift up your church's leaders that they may be empowered by the Holy Spirit. Pray for a spirit of power that your church will not be tempted to compromise.

Chapter 6
Company Widow Discovers Oil!

1. This widow felt she was helpless to change her fate. We feel the same way sometimes. Why do we feel this way when we serve a God who's power is limitless?
2. Read Psalm 51:10-12. What takes away the joy of God's salvation to create what Haslam calls a "mood of loss" in believers?
3. What religious fads have you witnessed that have either passed away already, or certainly will?
4. Read 2 Timothy 1:7. What are some circumstances that cause Christians to fear, when God's Word teaches us that fear is not from God?
5. List some ways in which the local church is in need of change, but its own denial keeps that change from happening.
6. In what ways are our prayers different when we are desperate and when we are calm and unruffled?
7. Think of a time when you or someone you know prayed for something and what God did in response was much greater than what you had imagined. What limited the original prayer?
8. What are some ways in which oil has been used as a symbol for the Holy Spirit?
9. What parts of the story of this widow show you her faith?
10. What will you need faith to face in the next few weeks?

Prayer Focus: Ask God to fill you with joy that others will recognize as spiritual joy. Expect power from God to change your world.

Chapter 7
How to Raise a Dead Kid

1. What are the challenges of raising children in today's world?
2. If you could change society in any way to make child rearing easier and more effective what would you change?
3. How can the church best help parents?
4. The Shunammite woman showed love to Elisha in down-to-earth, practical ways. Describe a time when someone showed you love in that way.
5. Think of someone who has the gift of hospitality. What are the telltale signs?
6. It seems there is always *something* else that we want. How can we become content with our lives the way this woman was?
7. Haslam states, "Many parents give their children everything except themselves." What are the contributing factors to relationships where this is true?
8. Even though her son was dead, this woman went to great lengths to help her son. What examples have you seen of a parent's faith and love taking him or her great distances or through great difficulties for their child?
9. What kinds of strict propriety have you witnessed that harmed rather than helped a child's faith?
10. If influencing children is so important (and it is), why is it often difficult to recruit children's workers in the church?

Prayer Focus: Remember in prayer today all the parents and children's workers in your church. Pray for God to permeate their homes and their children's lives.

Chapter 8
When the Church Gets into a Stew

1. In what ways do you think the church is like a battleship?
2. Think of a time when you experienced God's grace. What was it like?
3. Elisha showed God's grace through his own generosity. Describe a time when you've seen someone do the same thing.
4. Haslam quoted, "Faith needs a catastrophe to walk on." What does that mean based on your experience?
5. Why do you think life can be such a struggle?
6. We often make promises we don't intend to keep when we are in a crisis. Why is it so easy to forget those promises?
7. The gourds poisoned the stew. They made it no good. What kinds of reactions and interactions poison the situations around you that should be filled with grace?
8. Describe a time when God's grace came to you or someone you know in the form of protection from danger.
9. Think of someone who finds joy in giving. What makes it easy for him or her, when others find it so difficult?
10. Which of your resources would you like to see multiplied so that you could give more away?

Prayer Focus: Thank God for the grace He has given you and your family—including protection, provision, peace in trials, and miracles.

Chapter 9
For the First Time in Your Life Feel Really Clean

1. What are some conditions in your culture that have shame

attached to them the same as leprosy did in Naaman's culture?

2. Have you ever witnessed a healing or experienced one in your own life? Describe it.

3. Think about the "but" in your life, the one thing that is a disappointment no matter how good your life gets. What would you give up in order to get rid of that "but"?

4. What gave the servant girl the grace to help her captors?

5. Naaman carried a letter from the king hoping it would help him obtain God's blessing. What kinds of things do we do in the hope that we will receive God's blessing, favor, or approval?

6. Why are we often more comfortable paying our way than receiving a gift?

7. Naaman wanted to be healed, yet at first refused to bathe in the Jordan. Why do we sometimes do the same thing, wanting our lives to be different, yet not being willing to do what it takes to make them different?

8. What is something God has asked of you or someone you know that required swallowing your pride?

9. Why do you think Elisha would take nothing from Naaman?

Prayer Focus: Thank God for the free gift of salvation and, in humility, ask God to take away the "leprosy" in your life.

Chapter 10

The Man Who Let Slip on Reality

1. How can a person like Gehazi be so closely associated with a godly man like Elisha and yet still be mercenary in his outlook?

2. Read 1 Timothy 5:17-18. It is certainly not wrong for vocational ministers to receive compensation for their work. Why

didn't Gehazi's actions fit in this category?

3. Read Colossians 3:23. Gehazi took matters into his own hands because he doubted his employer's decision. How could we apply this verse to a similar situation?

4. It often becomes easy to deceive when we feel we've been short-changed or wronged. Are there mitigating circumstances that justify dishonesty like Gehazi's? Why or why not?

5. In what ways do you think Gehazi's punishment fit his crime?

6. Why do you think Gehazi chose to include Elisha in his lie to Naaman?

7. Most of us have violated or felt we violated our integrity at some point. What kind of feeling or struggles do you associate with that violation?

8. How do you think Elisha felt when he knew what Gehazi had done? Why?

9. What does it take to restore a relationship that has been hurt like Gehazi's and Elisha's?

10. What does it take to be used of God again after we slip or violate our integrity?

Prayer Focus: Ask God for strength to overcome when you face evil that could rob you of your destiny—your calling and ministry.

Chapter 11
Have You Lost Your Edge Lately?

1. Sometimes good suggestions come from unexpected people. What kind of battle goes on inside of you at those times?

2. How do we find a balance between wanting to give the best to God in terms of buildings and resources and not overextending our budgets of time and money?

3. How would you explain luck to someone unfamiliar with the concept?
4. What is the difference, if any, between fate and destiny?
5. Is there such a thing as a self-fulfilling prophecy? What is it to you?
6. What are the arguments (on both sides) regarding accidents or circumstances in life that happen by chance? Are there such things, or is there a purpose in everything?
7. Read Romans 8:28-29. How does this Scripture fit in with your view of fate?
8. Think about a time when you or someone you know realized that their actions or ministry had lost effectiveness. What did they do about it?
9. In thinking of this story as an illustration of the influence of our ministries or actions, what might have kept that young prophet from going to Elisha to admit he had lost his edge and to get help?
10. In which of your endeavors do you most want God's power (the ax-head) to stay sharp and intact?

Prayer Focus: Praise God for the times He has restored you spiritually, emotionally, physically, mentally.

Chapter 12
Help—We're Surrounded

1. In what ways does your life sometimes feel like a war movie?
2. In regard to Ben-Hadad, Haslam states, "We come to resemble what we most worship." How have you seen that true in your own life or the lives around you?
3. Elijah gained enemies by doing what was right. In what ways does that still happen today?
4. What kinds of circumstances can make you fearful?

5. If we could see the angelic dimension around us, what do you think we would see?

6. If you had been the king of Israel when Elisha delivered the men of Aram directly into his hands, what would your reaction have been?

7. If we could incorporate Elisha's perspective into our lives, that our accomplishments belong first to God, how might that change the way we view our enemies and our competitors?

8. Think of the person that most resembles an enemy to you. How can you show him or her mercy?

9. Why is it easier to show mercy when we are fully founded in the truth of God's power and protection?

Prayer Focus: Pray that in your ministry, when Satan is attacking you, God will give you faith to stop panicking and trust in Him.

Chapter 13
Who Has Believed the Report of the Lord?

1. What are some of the most notable acts of aggression from history?

2. What are some of the evidences of the moral decline in our own culture?

3. At times, the repentance of a leader, religious or political, can make us uncomfortable. Why is that?

4. Read Romans 2:3-4. How does this verse relate to Elisha's three voices of rebuke, hope, and judgment?

5. The four lepers initiated change because they decided they had nothing to lose in trying. Describe a time when you or someone you know have been freed up to make a decision because of this "nothing to lose" logic.

6. What would your reaction have been had you walked into

the deserted camp as these lepers did?

7. Often the only difference between a crazy action and a daring action is the outcome. Describe a time when you witnessed something you thought was crazy, only to find that it worked and was a brave, daring thing to do?

8. How often do you think we miss blessings from God because we are too cautious?

9. Why do we sometimes keep the news of Christ to ourselves?

Prayer Focus: Request from God boldness in evangelism. And that you will become a catalyst for spiritual growth and revival in your church and community.

Chapter 14
Is There a Prophet in the House?

1. Think of someone you know who you believe has the gift of prophecy. What does that person offer the church?

2. Haslam states, "Truth cuts both ways." How have you witnessed this in your experience?

3. Most of us have heard state-fair fortunetellers or TV psychics or read fortune cookies that give such general prophecies that they could apply to anyone. What are some examples of these kinds of general statements?

4. How do you determine the difference, if any, between a coincidence and God's timely intervention?

5. The Shunammite woman received justice, but it was still up to her to go and ask for it. In what ways do you need to go and ask for justice in your day-to-day world?

6. Does there come a time when God's judgment cannot be stopped even by repentance? Why or why not?

7. How can we tell when we are being chastened by God?

8. Why is it such a typical reaction to turn to God in the worst

of times even when we have not developed a habit of depending on Him?

9. Have you ever prayed for healing? What were the results?

Prayer Focus: Pray for God's prophecy to be made known to your church today. Be prepared to be obedient.

Chapter 15
Our Victory in Death

1. When a good person who has made a great difference in our lives or in the world becomes terminally ill, what kinds of thoughts and questions are raised in our minds?
2. What does it mean to "die well"?
3. How would you like to spend your last years of life?
4. How would you like to be remembered after you die?
5. What would you have said if you had been asked to give the eulogy at Elisha's funeral?
6. What is the connection between our private prayer life and the power of our daily lives?
7. How can we build up our faith so that we won't limit God's ability to use us?
8. When you see Elisha in heaven, what will you ask or tell him?
9. Think of someone who influenced your life greatly when he or she was alive. In what ways does that person still influence your life today?
10. What kind of legacy of your own do you hope to be investing in this week?

Prayer Focus: Give praise to God for the opportunity to live a life of purpose and meaning and to die a death of victory.

INDEX OF LIFE ISSUES

Note: Page numbers sometimes refer to a relevant passage that continues for several pages.